DATE			
			SEP - 9 2003
FEB 11 2001	JUL 18 2001	MAR 29 2011	
FEB 27	AUG - 6 2001	AUG 23 2011	
	2001 AUG 28 2001		
MAR 24	2001		
JUL 11	2001 SEP 22 2001		
		JUN 23 2002	
APR 17 2001			
APR 26 2001	JUN 20 2003		
MAY - 8 2001	AUG 19 2003		
JUN 23 2001			

Every Day
I Love You More

(just not today)

Lessons in Loving
One Partner for Life

Every Day
I Love
You More

(just not today)

Nancy Shulins

WARNER BOOKS

A Time Warner Company

Warner Books, Inc., 1271 Avenue of the Americas, New York, NY 10020
Visit our Web site at www.twbookmark.com

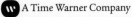 A Time Warner Company

Printed in the United States of America

First Printing: January 2001

10   9   8   7   6   5   4   3   2   1

Library of Congress Cataloging-in-Publication Data

Shulins, Nancy.
    Every day I love you more : just not today / by Nancy Shulins.
        p. cm.
    ISBN 0-446-52551-0
    1. Marriage.   2. Man-woman relationships.   3. Love.
    4. Intimacy (Psychology)   I. Title.

HQ734 .S586 2001
306.7—dc21   00-032494

For Mark

Every Day
I Love You More

(just not today)

Introduction

A woman of forty-seven who has been married
twenty-seven years and has six children knows what love
really is and once described it for me like this:
"Love is what you have been through with somebody."

JAMES THURBER

We grow up believing we know all about love. After all, who among us doesn't love our parents, our siblings, our pals, and our pets? By the time we reach voting age, most of us have experienced at least some semblance of romantic love: the pounding heart, the sweaty palms, the libido on overdrive, the overwhelming intensity, the inevitable broken heart. But no matter. One day, we are taught, we will gaze across a crowded room and into the eyes of our intended, our one and only, our other half, the person with whom we'll live happily ever after, in sickness and in health, until death do us part.

Once we get home, though, and the clink of champagne glasses is replaced by the dishwasher's hum, we find we're just another couple peering across a dining room table wondering if we've done the right thing. Because grown-up love, for the most part, owes far less to fate than the movies would have us believe. The fact is, there's no one person out there who's perfect, no "other half" destined to complete us. Instead, there are any number of people with whom we could no doubt find happiness, from that freckle-faced kid with the wide, goofy grin who sat next to us in second grade to the tall, lanky guy with the geriatric schnauzer we always flirt with at the park.

For most of us, it's largely a matter of timing and the person who happens to be there when the music stops and it's time to sit down. When our best friend gets married. When our sister gives birth. When we decide we really *do* like bone china. Something feels right, so we make a commitment. Not to just anyone, of course, but to a kind, loving person with warm eyes and a wonderful laugh. Someone we care about who cares about us. Someone whose soul fits with ours.

My own "crowded room" was a bustling newsroom in New York, the world headquarters of the Associated Press. That's where my husband and I locked eyes for the first time over a computer terminal sixteen years ago. His were brown and incredibly soft; they were also bloodshot as hell—not just from staring at that electronic screen, but from months of working from midnight to eight. Since I was working days, I still have no idea what twist of fate brought us to the office at the same time that once. Our conflicting schedules helped fan the flames after that as we stole moments between his shift and mine. Most courtships benefit from an obstacle or two; the struggle to surmount them is an ideal dress rehearsal for overcoming life's troubles as a team.

Not that either of us gave real life much thought as we unpacked our wedding gifts at home. And what newlywed couple ever does? Everything seems so shiny and perfect and new. We put away the china, mail our thank-you notes or change-of-address cards, and get ready to happily grow old together.

Over time, though, things crop up that make us less sure of our choices, a daily onslaught of things we didn't count on, like illness and conflicts, domestic disasters and debts. The stuff of reality comes at us from every direction. It takes its toll on our relationships and our psyches because it's so inconsistent with our fantasies. In the fairy tales, every day after the wedding is compressed into a single line: "And so they lived happily ever after." And yet none of us do, not exactly. We live happily on some days and horribly on others. Mostly, we live somewhere in the middle, never in quite the same place.

But despite the gap between fantasy and reality, some people do manage to live happily, when everything is said and done. They're the ones who see love as a process, as something they've learned how to do, through humor, sensitivity, kindness, flexibility, tolerance, patience, and more. As with all of life's teachings, these lessons take a long time to master, but that only strengthens the magic. In the end, lasting love is more extraordinary than even the poets profess, because it's something you and your mate teach each other, bit by bit, day by day, year by year. You explore all its facets together, including the ones you don't think of as love until later, the ones that surprise you every time. All are woven together, airtight, overlapping, a layer for each day and night. In the end, what you have is far richer than any fairy tale you've ever read. It's as complex and wondrous as life.

Long marriages run in my family. My parents took their vows fifty-one years ago; my grandparents, more than seventy. My grandmother continues to keep count even though her husband has been dead twenty years. Regardless, she says, she still *feels* married. She still keeps his birthday on the calendar and his raincoat in the closet, along with two pairs of neatly ironed pajamas, and ties that now look much too wide.

In the hope of building an equally strong bond in my marriage, I began talking to my grandmother about hers. And to others—my mother, my sister, my friends; then to their friends, their mothers, and so on. Nobody had all the answers, but everyone had one or two. And by weaving their wisdom together, I began to see how it just might be possible to condense a lifetime's worth of lessons into a single book, one that might help explain how to feel truly married, regardless of what comes our way.

The essays on these pages blend stories from my marriage with those of my family and friends, along with bits of advice and practical suggestions applicable to us all. Most were written outdoors at an old picnic table with my curious horse looking on, a cat or two in my lap, and the wind in my hair, which may account for the breeziness of the tone. It is midwinter now as I write these last words, and the paddocks are knee-deep in snow. Married life, like the seasons, is always in flux; soft breezes give way to stiff winds. But I have already seen the first buds on the trees, and my horse is beginning to shed. Like restaurant hash and the coming of spring, grown-up love must be taken on faith. You don't need me to tell you how hard that can be. It's my hope that these stories will help.

—Nancy Shulins

There are only two ways to live your life.

One is as though nothing is a miracle.

The other is as though everything is a miracle.

ALBERT EINSTEIN

I
T WAS SIXTEEN years ago tonight, January 29, 1985,
when the big, bearded man in the dirty beige parka
picked me up for our first-ever date. It was a cold Tuesday evening, although we pretended it was Saturday, a
little trick we perfected during the years I worked week-
days and he worked nights and weekends. On that first
night in New York, we ate Indian food at a hole-in-the-
wall, then walked around the city, stopping for drinks
every now and then to thaw out. Mostly, we talked—
about life, work, ourselves—and we kept right on talking until the buses had stopped running and I had to
take a cab home. Just before we said good night, we
walked down a side street, past a bakery. The place was
closed, but the display window was all lit up, and we
paused to check out the fancy, overpriced goodies.

That's when we saw it, on top of a linzer torte: the fattest mouse in Manhattan trapped inside the window, happily gorging away. The last of our first-date nervousness melted away as we stood there and laughed like hyenas. We still do, whenever one of us brings it up. It was an arresting sight, incongruous and rare, not unlike finding love on a side street at two in the morning in a city of eight million souls.

We've been celebrating that cold winter's night ever since, with candlelit dinners and long, moonlit walks, smarmy cards and champagne and tandoori, along with the occasional marzipan mouse. And while we also observe our wedding anniversary with similarly romantic gestures, I think we look forward to this even more. Because, unlike our wedding day, a day we orchestrated, planned, and rehearsed to the letter, January 29 simply happened, due to forces beyond our control. And as it unfolded, on a cold Tuesday night, the ordinary became extraordinary: the wondrous, mysterious, marvelous—a miracle, in other words.

If you think you have yet to experience a miracle, perhaps it's time to rethink what that means. The miracle that brought you and your soul mate together is the best place I know to start. Once a year, why not give it a night all its own? To look back in wonder. To give fate its due. To lift your glass to the forces that joined you.

I believe a little incompatibility is the spice of life, particularly if he has income and she is pattable.

OGDEN NASH

SHORTLY BEFORE WE fall head over heels, some of us have a curious habit: we list the pros and cons of prospective suitors on paper to see if a romance makes sense. It may seem cold and calculating, but I suspect it's nothing more than our heads trying to govern our hearts. It's also wildly unreliable, as my husband and I can attest. If you were to put us on paper, here's how we'd look:

He likes: nights out on the town, staying up till all hours, dressing down, electronic mail, late-night suppers, riding bikes.

She likes: quiet evenings at home, rising before dawn, dressing up, handwritten notes, early dinners, riding horses.

You get the idea. On paper we're oil and water, Israel and Palestine, Hatfield and McCoy. But couples don't live their lives on paper, which is why we're still married after fifteen long years: almost forever in dog years—and to us, on occasion, as well. Long enough to anticipate each other's lines before we say them and to feel mildly annoyed when we turn out to be right. It happened again just the other day when we were turning our king-size mattress, as we do every six months or so, whenever our bed starts to feel like a hammock. "I hate that dust ruffle," said my husband, and I said, "I *knew* you were going to say that." Then he straightened up, catching the edge of my night stand with his elbow and spilling a glass of cider all over my book. "You shouldn't have left it there," the man of my dreams said. And I said, "I *knew* you were going to say that."

I might have left it at that a few years ago, but nowadays, it seems, I know better. I know better because once, when I called him at work to tell him I'd just backed out of the driveway and into the stone wall beside it, his first question wasn't "How could you do something so stupid?" but, rather, "Are you okay?" I knew he was going to say that, too. And when I paged him that time in New Orleans minutes after he'd arrived from New York and told him the ultrasound showed we were having another miscarriage instead of a baby, I knew just what he'd say before he said it: that he'd be catching the next plane back home.

It occurred to me then that nowhere is it written that one annoying, predictable line need follow another. We all have the power to rewrite the script, to opt *not* to punch someone's buttons. Should you find yourself having the same tired argument with your mate, toss out a new line and watch yourselves rewrite the ending. Push your annoyance aside and remember a time when he said what you needed to hear, just as you knew he would: Hang in there, honey. I'm on my way home.

And so, many years later, as I tossed him a towel to mop up the cider I shouldn't have left there in the first place, I added, "You're right. And I'm sorry." Whereupon my beloved informed me he knew I was going to say that. He then grinned like a maniac and snapped my butt with the towel.

He missed me by a mile.

The only time a woman really succeeds in changing a man is when he is a baby.

NATALIE WOOD

AFTER A DECADE of dating shy, silent types who drove vintage VWs and wore getups that made mockeries of their trust funds, my sister fell for a bona fide oddball. He was a loud, penniless, overbearing film student from Staten Island who transported her to and from dates on the handlebars of an ancient delivery bike. The first time I met him, he had on jeans and a bowler, and he never shut up for a second. The three of us had lunch at a diner in Vermont, where he made bad puns and laughed uproariously in a voice that bounced off the mountains and rattled the spoons. I looked across the table at my sister for some sign that his behavior was unusual, a nervous response to meeting one of her relatives, but she was oblivious. I couldn't have been more shocked had she showed up with a Pygmy, but I figured, what the heck. It wasn't as if she were gonna *marry* the guy.

It was a lovely wedding. I was looking at the pictures the other day, thinking about how little my brother-in-law has changed in the twenty years since he married my sister. He's lost most of his hair, but he still has the bowler, and if he fails to dominate a family gathering, we all worry that he's getting sick. My family adores him, a diamond in the rough who's retained his rough edges despite my sister's vigorous attempts at grinding them down. She doesn't much bother anymore. They have two kids now, and as she says, there are only so many hours in a day.

When did oblivion give way to self-consciousness about his little behavioral quirks? I can't pinpoint the moment, but I believe it was after they made the decision to wed. His behavior suddenly became a reflection of her, and that drastically altered her view. It's one of the ironies of life that those of us who lose our hearts to men who wear bowlers and tell corny jokes invariably expend a great deal of effort—we're talking pyramid-building effort here—trying to remodel them into shy, silent types. Construction begins the moment we realize we're too smitten to keep them under wraps. No, sooner or later there's bound to be an unveiling, and chances are it won't be very pretty. The notion of subjecting our oddball to the scrutiny of our other significant others—parents! girlfriends! employers!—unleashes nightmares of epic proportion. It also rekindles fears of rejection seldom experienced since our prom. Seismic shifts in perspective occur as we cease to regard the object of our affection with our own loving eyes but, rather, with the gaze of some demented critic, a critic who sees before her not some brilliant iconoclast with his own sense of style but a geek in a very bad hat.

So, out comes the heavy equipment. Ground is broken and the project begins. Months—even years—later, we pause to assess what our struggles have wrought: exhaustion (ours); hurt feelings (his). And for the most part, not a hell of a lot else. In the meantime, most of our nearest and dearest have long since fallen for the same quirky traits we once did. As for those who have yet to be dazzled, we have long since ceased to worry. Or care.

The moral, of course, is that no one's more critical or less forgiving of our partners than we are, so we may as well get off their case. Let your mind wander back to those long-ago days when introducing him over lunch was a joy, when he seemed so much more than the shy, silent types you went out with before he showed up. "Find" that long-lost neon plaid shirt he's so fond of, the one you've kept buried in your underwear drawer. Take a sentimental journey on the handlebars of his bike. Let him tell his beloved joke in mixed company— or, better yet, urge him to tell it. Watch his face flush and his eyes shine as his audience howls at the punch line. Catch a glimpse, sweet and fleeting, of the oddball you married.

Make him promise you he'll never change.

> Marriage should, I think, always be a little hard and
> new and strange. It should be breaking your shell and
> going into another world, and a bigger one.
>
> ANNE MORROW LINDBERGH

WHEN MY HUSBAND and I were first dating, we used to order Chinese from a little carryout place around the corner from his Brooklyn apartment. I still remember the first time we did this, because it taught me something about myself that embarrasses me to this day.

We were sitting together on his sofa going over the menu, which featured a number of spicy dishes printed in red. "I don't eat spicy food," I informed my then-boyfriend. When he asked me why not, I looked up at him blankly. I thought a minute, then explained that I wasn't brought up with it so I'd never gotten into the habit, which sounded lame even to me. I was, after all, more than thirty years old. I watched him circle several red-letter dishes and reach for the phone, thinking, Oh, well. I wasn't that hungry any-way.

The food arrived a half hour later. When the first cautious bite didn't kill me, I took another. And another. After three or four bites, I began to enjoy the sensation of fiery heat in my mouth. After a few more, I found myself craving it. I ended up packing it in like a farmhand, my diet and my taste for the mild and bland both irrevocably shot to hell.

It's a pattern we've repeated many times in our marriage, with numerous other things I thought I didn't like, from camping trips to science fiction, action-adventure films to red wine, hiking to alternative rock. I, in turn, introduced my husband to dress clothes, fresh flowers, heavy metal, and dog ownership. When we first met, he'd never set foot in a four-star restaurant, and I'd never played backgammon. And while I still won't eat sushi, and he still hates Metallica, we have managed to broaden each other's horizons in myriad unforeseen ways, a key aspect of any relationship that's to last us the rest of our lives.

It can be pretty scary to follow your mate into the deep, murky waters of change. But a little discomfort is not only tolerable, it's desirable, because it means you're moving beyond the status quo. For years my mother-in-law and her husband longed to travel to Europe, but her fear of flying kept them at home. She finally got tired of looking at everyone else's vacation slides and took a course offered by one of the airlines for people who are afraid to fly. By pushing herself beyond her "comfort zone," she conquered her phobia and stretched the boundaries of her marriage as well. And while she's still nervous while airborne, she no longer lets her fear stop her from exploring exotic new lands. She and her husband have jetted off to Italy and France and look forward to many more journeys.

As for me, I look forward to red-letter days filled with spicy heat and Szechuan Shrimp. The partnerships that stay fresh are the challenging ones, the ones that never stop pushing us out of our ruts, coaxing us to shut our eyes, take a deep breath, and soar.

Some things . . . arrive in their own mysterious hour,

on their own terms and not yours,

to be seized or relinquished forever.

GAIL GODWIN

EVERY RELATIONSHIP, every marriage, has its magical moments, moments that affirm and define us as couples, moments that make our hearts soar. They come at odd hours, like babies: during blizzards or when there's nothing on TV. We'll be reading the Sunday paper, driving somewhere in the car, or just making dinner together, when *wham!* something happens that results in a deepening sense of connection, followed by a rush of pure joy. A song we played constantly during our courtship comes over the radio, magically transporting us both back in time. I tell him a joke that makes us laugh till we cry—not because it's so funny, but because I tell it so badly. I'll glance over at him in the kitchen, stirring broth into the pot of risotto, and he'll look to me just as he did when our relationship was brand-new. In my mind's eye, I'll be back in his Brooklyn apartment, watching him cook for me for the first time, wondering if I've finally met my match, hoping upon hope that I have . . .

We can't make them happen, these cosmic moments, when the planets align and all's right with our world. We can only recognize and savor them when they do. At the same time, we can create a climate in which they're more apt to occur. By treating each other with kindness and respect. By anticipating and responding to each other's needs. By paying attention to the little things that turn an average day into a great one. By loving each other more every day.

A wise woman once told me that staying happily married for life depends on the ability to fall in love, over and over, with the same person. That's what these special moments do for us; they allow us to reexperience the act of falling in love. And the more often we experience them, the happier we are, which is why so many of us ritualistically return to the restaurant where we had our first dinner together or the inn where we spent our first night.

Most of us have albums that enable us to relive our weddings whenever we choose; some of us even captured the ceremony on videotape. But what about all the cosmic moments that follow, the moments in which we find ourselves falling in love with the same person all over again? Wouldn't it be just as wonderful to be able to relive them at will?

Nancy Shulins

Today, start preserving your relationship's magical moments by writing them down in a marriage album. Buy a beautiful diary, blank book, or calendar, and begin describing and dating your moments. Feel free to include illustrations or photos, or anything else that helps tell the story, keeping in mind that your words may one day be read by your children, your children's children, and so on. Unlike your wedding album, which records the events of a single day—a day quite unlike any you had experienced before or have since—the marriage album will be a treasury of the special moments that take place between you after the honeymoon ends. And while your wedding album is all about fantasy, your marriage album will be all about love. Real love. The kind that grows deeper and stronger with time.

Arrange whatever pieces

come your way.

VIRGINIA WOOLF

M Y FRIEND JANICE wrecked her car the other day. She swerved to avoid an oncoming car that had drifted over into her lane and went off the road, through the guardrail, and down an embankment. A stone wall finally stopped her, rupturing her gas tank and filling her car with smoke and fumes. Miraculously enough, the accident left her with only a slight case of whiplash and a pounding heart, which is to say nothing of what it did to her boyfriend, who arrived on the scene to flashing lights, the car's mangled carcass, and no sign whatsoever of Janice.

"I was sure she was lying in an ambulance on her way to the hospital," John said later. That instant of not knowing will stay with him forever, an instant of fearing the worst. He choked on his heart as he ran to the cop car. "Where is she? Where is she?" In fact, she was huddled in the back of the cruiser, with a perfect view of her love's frantic face.

Since he'd had to work, she'd scheduled a busy day too, but suddenly none of these activities seemed important. They ended up canceling everything and going home together instead. And by the time darkness fell, she'd begun to recover from the terrible shock of it all. But there was also this: "We seem so much closer," she told me when I called to find out how she was. "We've both been so busy doing our own thing that we had sort of drifted apart." An oncoming car, a moment of terror, and they'd crashed into each other's arms. "That look on his face," she said softly. "I'll never forget it." And she won't.

I know that look. I have seen it myself on occasion: a lifetime of love and concern telescoped into an instant in which everything else falls away. It is primal and powerful, and I'll never forget either. Nor will anyone else who has seen it. It shouldn't take a near-disaster—or an actual one—to remind us of all that we have or to show us how quickly everything can be lost. Remember that tonight when your mate pulls into the driveway, home again, safe and sound, one more time.

My friend's neck is still sore, and her left hand still tingles. But that's not what she's focusing on. It's that look on John's face. The safety of his arms. The closeness that's born of close calls.

**Life has taught us that love does not consist
in gazing at each other but in looking
outward together in the same direction.**

ANTOINE DE SAINT-EXUPÉRY

T HE STARS ARE out tonight. I would have missed
them completely had my husband not cut me off
in midsentence, pulled the car over, pointed up at the
sky, and said, "Look." I was more than a little put out
with him at the time for having disrupted my diatribe
on the slimeball who'd stolen a parking space out from
under me earlier in the day. Then I saw what he was
pointing at. Oh, my.

It is hard to be petty while gazing up at the stars.
It's also hard to be angry or cranky or mean, or anything other than awestruck. The stars have a way of
putting you in your place. They have done this for us
many times in our marriage, on warm summer
evenings and cold winter nights, interrupting our
squabbles, refereeing our fights, and generally butting

into our lives with a late-breaking bulletin from the cosmos: Hey, you two! Get *over* yourselves!

It's embarrassing to admit it, but I tend not to notice the Milky Way on my own. Earthbound by nature, I'm scared of heights, anxious on airplanes, and prone to recurring nightmares in which I tumble out of the sky. I often walk with my head down, oblivious to anything above the tree line. A lone crocus or woolly caterpillar can stop me in my tracks, yet eclipses and comets blow right by me. I truly dislike what this suggests about me, that I'm reductive and cautious and overly pessimistic. I may be reading entirely too much into a metaphor, but then again, possibly not. After all, it's tough to soar with the eagles if you refuse to let your feet leave the ground.

My other half is just the opposite. A sailor who loves science fiction, he's forever scanning the heavens for clues to tomorrow's weather or signs of some alien force. An optimist who believes that the sky is the limit, he's always dragging me outside at night, pointing out pinpricks of light from the past that instantly change my perspective: from the center of the universe to an infinitesimal speck, a much healthier view in the long run. It's a neat trick, and one that works equally well on my husband. In fact, I daresay it could work on us all. I defy anyone to feel consumed with his own self-importance after even a brief interlude of gazing at the stars. And I defy any couple to stargaze without reaching out for each other, *two* infinitesimal specks huddled together against the vastness of infinite space.

Every Day I Love You More

What's more, unlike most other mind-altering substances, stars are widely available, legal, and free, although I do recommend such optional extras as a hot tub, a hammock, or a quilt. Bear in mind that champagne marries perfectly with the night sky. It's like having your own private glassful of stars.

Some say life is the thing,

but I prefer reading.

RUTH RENDELL

COLIN AND GINA met at their college library when she dropped the last volume of *Remembrance of Things Past* on his foot. Two Proust lovers alone in the stacks on a Tuesday. It was meant to be, and they both knew it. They cut class and went out for tea.

Colin, a newspaper editor who writes short stories in his spare time and collects beautifully written paragraphs the way some men collect autographed baseballs, has never doubted that Gina was The One. A tall, willowy blonde I've never once seen in pants, Gina has a dreamy, romantic quality that brings old-fashioned literary heroines to mind and mesmerizes the high school boys who crowd into her English lit classes. The conversation she and Colin started that Tuesday has been at the center of their lives ever since, a wide-ranging dialogue about characters, narratives, and plots.

And twenty years after that first cup of tea, Gina and Colin's romance continues unabated, as does their passionate love affair with the well-written word: biographies, novels, short stories, and poems. Colin often has two or three books going at once, while Gina prefers to polish off the complete works of one writer before moving on to another. But regardless of all that they read on their own, they always have something they're reading together, chapter by chapter, night after night. I know plenty of folks who read to their children, but Colin and Gina are the only adults I know who take turns reading aloud to each other.

They've been at it for years, every night after dinner, a ritual they find much more satisfying than "must-see" TV. It's also more intimate, according to Gina, who says they often bring their book to bed with them and one reads the other to sleep, though they're just as likely to stay up half the night talking. "We start off talking about the characters, but invariably we wind up discussing ourselves," Gina says. "The way we react to stories, how we feel about individual characters—these things are very revealing. And having gotten into the habit of talking every night, we tend to have fewer problems between us, because we pick up on them right away, before small issues become big ones."

Today, take a few minutes to jot down a few of your all-time favorite books, and ask your partner to do the same. Compare lists and try to pinpoint where your tastes and interests intersect. Perhaps you both love a good Agatha Christie mystery, or a supernatural thriller à la Stephen King. If you can't find common ground, take your separate lists to a library or bookstore and ask for some recommendations on books that fall somewhere in between. Or look at titles that correspond to some shared hobby or passion: food memoirs for cooks or true-life adventures for sailors. Choose something you both find appealing and start reading a chapter a night to each other, perhaps at bedtime or over dessert, and share with your lover the transcendent pleasures of the printed page. "Learn to love good books," Robert Ingersoll once wrote. "There are treasures in books that all the money in the world cannot buy, but that the poorest laborer can have for nothing."

**More than kisses,
letters mingle souls.**

JOHN DONNE

I F MY HOUSE were on fire, here's what I would save:
our wedding album (actual proof I was once a size
four), my grandmother's handwritten recipes for her
Old World specialties (none of which I've been able to
duplicate), my collection of priceless original artwork
(my nieces' and nephews' garishly crayoned drawings of
my horse), and a half-dozen sheets of lined paper
ripped out of a notebook, covered in red ink that's
starting to fade. My husband's love letters, circa 1985.

There are three in all, enough to last me a lifetime—
a good thing, considering he hasn't written one since.
In all fairness, though, that's not entirely true; it's not
that husbands stop writing love letters, exactly. It's just
that they tend to look somewhat different from the
kind boyfriends write. Take the one I received just last
week, on a memo pad I found on the table: "Hon: Please

be VERY CAREFUL driving to the barn. The roads could be slippery. Me." Or how about this one, penned in green on the back of a Chinese menu left by the phone: "Started the laundry and took videos back. Here's some $$$. Don't worry about dinner. I'll pick something up." They don't have quite the same ring as "How do I love thee? Let me count the ways. . . ." On the other hand, when you come right down to it, aren't they basically saying the same thing?

Still, I do miss the other kind, those letters that deserve to be read for their poetry as well as their declarations of love. Like the playful prose of poet Ogden Nash, in this letter to his future wife, Frances: "Have you heard that I love you? I'm not sure that I made it clear to you, and I don't want to have a misunderstanding. It's such a young love yet—just nine and a half months old, born November thirteenth, 1928 at about nine o'clock in the evening. But it's big for its age, and seems much older. . . . This is a particularly gifted and intelligent pen. Look what it's writing now: I love you."

Or consider this steamy dispatch from Napoléon, who was not so busy conquering Europe that his mind didn't occasionally wander: "A kiss on your heart," he wrote Joséphine, "and then one a little lower down, much lower down."

Few of us bother with letters anymore; even fewer with love letters to our mates. We say we're too busy, and yet, think of Napoléon. If he could find time, so can we. Perhaps the thought of drafting a love letter summons painful memories of freshman composition, of drifting aimlessly in a sea of crumpled paper, a half-chewed pencil stub in your mouth. If so, erase that image and replace it with that of the love of your life. What if this were your last chance to tell him what he means to you, what he has brought to your life? Picture that conversation, imagine the words you would use. Find a few quiet moments today and write these words down. List the highlights of your years together. Describe the attributes you love the most: a smile, a gesture, a laugh. Good for you; you've just written your first draft.

Sometime tomorrow, stitch these snippets together as gracefully and simply as you can, with a good pen on your best stationery. Spray it with your scent and tuck it into a matching envelope. Add a stamp and address, and drop it into the mailbox. Eagerly await your reply.

> **Ever since Eve gave Adam the apple,**
> **there has been a misunderstanding**
> **between the sexes about gifts.**

NAN ROBERTSON

MY HUSBAND GAVE me business cards for Christmas. And while he put a great deal of thought into them, debating the merits of this font or that and weighing the pros and cons of gray versus cream, the fact remains: he gave me business cards for Christmas. And even as he sat there, his face awash in anticipation as I hurriedly tore off the paper, my first thought when I opened the fancy blue box essentially came down to this: What the hell were you thinking?

I didn't say it out loud, of course, for the simple reason that he also gave me a bracelet, a book, and a saddle pad, and because he didn't say "What the hell were you thinking?" when I gave him stationery for Valentine's Day. Truth be told, he didn't say much at all. He just sat there in stunned silence, gazing sorrowfully down at the box. What was I thinking, indeed?

And yet, once we'd each taken a deep, cleansing breath—not to mention a much closer look, both gifts proved more thoughtful than they'd seemed at first glance. My husband knew I was experiencing an identity crisis, having left journalism to start writing books. The cards were his way of reminding me I still had a place in the world, despite the fact that my address had changed. And in my search for a gift for my seafaring mate, I'd been drawn to the stationery's abstract waves, and to the Robert Louis Stevenson poem about "blue days at sea" stenciled on the lid of the box. The box that, up until a moment ago, when I fetched it to reread the poem, was still sitting precisely where he'd left it the day I gave it to him.

Presents are tricky—eagerly awaited, highly prized, and occasionally fraught with peril. Like mirrors, they reflect the way others see us, as opposed to how we see ourselves, which explains how the silk camisole we were expecting becomes a big, fleecy sweatshirt instead, or how leather gloves become warm woolen mittens. However, explanations do not always make things OK, and the instant it takes to lift a lid off a box doesn't give us much time to regroup: to rearrange our expressions of disappointment or dismay and to choke out, "It's *just* what I wanted!"

No one can be expected to get it right all the time, but if your mate consistently misses the mark, it's time for an honest discussion. Keep in mind that just as sexual issues are best discussed outside the bedroom, so should conversations about what does and does not constitute a fabulous present take place far away from crumpled gift wrap and dried-out Christmas trees.

Once the venue's been set, put your cards on the table and don't waste any time being subtle. Direct is best, as in, "You know what I'd love you to get me?" Or, "I think a [fill in the blank] would be the greatest present in the world!" Do not ask for the moon, the Hope diamond, or a shiny new automobile. Make it something attainable, affordable, and appealing. Later on, once you've built up his confidence, there'll be plenty of time to ask for manure for rose bushes, or other intimidating specialty items. For now, keep it specific and simple, and don't forget to include sizes and color preferences.

And when the big day comes and he gives you your present—the present you requested, campaigned for, and described in excruciating, painstaking detail, act surprised. Act very surprised.

Listening, not imitation,

may be the sincerest form of flattery.

DR. JOYCE BROTHERS

HOW MANY TIMES has this happened to you: You're busy trying to pull dinner together when your sweetie walks into the kitchen and starts talking. You smile and nod, you "uh-huh" and "mmm-hmmm" at what you hope are appropriate moments, all the while continuing to chop, measure, pour, season, and sauté. You're rummaging in the fridge for the garlic when you suddenly become aware that your loved one is no longer talking; in fact, you can all but feel him glaring at the back of your head. You try to calculate how long he's been silent. You realize you haven't a clue. All you can do is pull your head out of the fridge, straighten up, and take your verbal licks like a man. "You're not listening," he says, sounding both accusing and wounded. "You're right," you say, sighing. "I'm sorry."

We often fail to give our partners our undivided attention, to really listen to them when they speak. During the early days of our courtships, most of us are so engrossed in each other that we tune out the rest of the world, the better to memorize every syllable and analyze every nuance. We are rapt. We are spellbound. We are golden retrievers at mealtime.

And then, somehow, we lose it. Those first magical days turn to weeks, months, and years. Through some slow and insidious process, the rest of the world eases back within earshot. It's our partners we start to tune out: "I *told* you that!" "You did not!" "Yes, I did. You never listen to me!"

Nothing's more gratifying than someone who listens. Really listens, patiently and intently, *actively,* the way psychiatrists, hairdressers, and hungry dogs do. "Most people never listen," Ernest Hemingway said, and he was right. If you doubt it, the next time your mate's filling you in on his day, try this experiment: Put down your knitting, your newspaper, your spatula, or your pen, look into his eyes, and give him your total attention, every iota, every ounce. He may get a bit flustered at first. Most people do; that's how unaccustomed we are to being heard. But once he recovers, he'll probably become more animated, more expressive. He'll square his shoulders and straighten his back, gaining stature both physically and psychically. In short, he'll be flattered—just as he was when you dated, when his words were a feast for your ears.

> I was in love with the whole world
> and all that lived in its rainy arms.

LOUISE ERDRICH

SAMANTHA HEADED WEST from Boston in a search for clean air, mountain streams, and adventure. She found all that and more on her two-week vacation. She also found love, the kind she never knew existed, the kind that's eluded her all her life.

Matthew is a third-year law student with blue eyes, sandy hair, and a passionate streak. He is funny and brilliant and kind. I haven't met him as yet, but I feel as if I had, as do most of Samantha's close friends. She has a habit of starting her sentences these days with, "You know what I love about Matthew?" Having met her for lunch a few hours ago, I now know dozens of things that she loves about Matthew: his sweetness, his intellect, his smile, and his charm, to say nothing of his love for her. I can also imagine what I was like years ago, when I first met my partner for life: preoccupied, giddy, giggly, and obsessed; in short, much like Samantha is now.

And while there are moments I wish she'd act like her old self, I find myself seeking her out. To borrow a cup of the stuff she exudes. To feel that old feeling again. To remind myself—and my husband—the feeling's still there, underneath all these layers of years. "You know what I love about Matthew?" Samantha asked me, dreamily sipping her glass of iced tea. "He loves the way I say 'Yeah.'" Then she said it and said it, again and again, experimenting with her inflection: "Yeah." *"Yeah."* "Yeah."

"You know what I love about my husband?" I asked, suddenly wanting to play the game, too. "The way he makes Michigan on his hand." Samantha looked at me blankly as I tried to explain how he uses the back of his hand as a map of the state where he'd lived before we met, pinpointing the location of various towns with the index finger of his other hand. I remembered when and where we had kissed the first time, on a Sunday in New York's Central Park. My nose started running a bit in the cold, and he handed me a white handkerchief. I thought about all the times he's done that since, how automatic that gesture's become. But that was the first time, and I was utterly charmed that he carried cotton instead of paper tissues. How many times have I laundered those squares? How many tears have I shed? All the highlights of my married life flooded back, countless moments of sorrow and joy. And all this because my friend has fallen in love. I was beginning to love Matthew, too.

God knows, love's first act doesn't last very long, though we feel its effects all our lives. Those first glossy hours stay with us forever, helping to keep us aloft, like the beaten egg whites folded into the batter to add lightness and height to a cake. While we tend to lose sight of them once they're whisked in, there are always those streaks that don't blend. They're the laughter that breaks through the stress on bad days; magic moments that transcend the years. But they'll never again look precisely the way that Samantha is seeing them now: lustrous and cloudlike and so full of air it's as though they will never deflate.

The smile that lights my friend's face as she speaks is as dazzling as beaten egg whites. "You know what I love about Matthew?" she asks, for the third time in less than an hour. And I smile back. Yeah. *Yeah.* Yeah.

A rock pile ceases to be a rock pile
the moment a single man contemplates it,
bearing within him the image of a cathedral.

ANTOINE DE SAINT-EXUPÉRY

AS I WRITE these words, I am sitting in the bright little room just off the living room that my husband and I loosely refer to as the sun room. At least we did until the bookshelves came down. For the purposes of this essay, I shall instead refer to it as the construction site, a description I fear may apply for some weeks.

What primal urge causes someone to tear apart a perfectly good room, a room that was just sitting there quietly minding its own p's and q's? An open, doorless room, clearly visible from the living room, that could now be described as an eyesore?

Where there were once built-in bookshelves and white cotton lace curtains, there is now unpainted stucco and naked windows without any sills. There is no stucco at all on the front wall. There are nailed-on plywood boards in its place. There also are books out the wazoo, stacked in teetering towers crammed up against the back wall. In other words, there is a mess.

What kind of person would do such a thing? A person with a router and radial arm saw in the basement. A person who feels right at home at Home Depot. A person with "vision." My spouse.

This is hardly an isolated incident. No sooner had we moved into our house when I caught him with a power drill in his hand. You think you know a guy. Once confronted, he made an excuse—"Do you want me to hang the window box or don't you?" I couldn't watch. Instead, I ran upstairs and placed a call to my sister-in-law, whose husband, my husband's brother, was busy remodeling their basement without a permit. "What should I do?" I wailed. "There's nothing you can do," she replied. "Suck it up. Learn how to live with it."

That was ten years ago, and I haven't learned yet. The outdoor stuff I can live with, but the inside jobs scare me to death. The rewiring projects. The window replacements. The drilling. The plumbing. The mess. If parents can lock out the Playboy Channel, why can't I program out *This Old House?*

He says the library will look so much better after he's finished remodeling it. He says it'll be bigger and brighter and nicer. He says I'll be thrilled with the change. The thing is, I probably will, just as I have been with everything else. But at the moment, I'm finding it less than aesthetically pleasing sitting here in my own hard-hat zone.

He says you can't make an omelette without breaking a few eggs.

In that case, I say, serve my eggs sunny-side up, in a room with some paint on the walls.

**Now join your hands,
and with your hands your hearts.**

SHAKESPEARE

IT HAD BEEN one of those dreary weekends that seem to go on for weeks, the kind that make Mondays look good. A cold, icy rain had been falling since Friday, and by Sunday afternoon we were surrounded by the flotsam and jetsam of two days' worth of ruined plans. My riding boots stood empty by the front door, my husband's sailing charts lay in a heap on the table, and we were beginning to snipe at each other. We found ourselves in sudden need of a marriage counselor, a quick trip to the tropics, a week at a spa. None of these being an option, we went instead to a movie. And our marriage was saved once again.

If every couple in America saw a movie a month, I'm convinced the divorce rate would plummet—provided, of course, they always held hands. We have been reaching for each other's hand in the dark ever since our second date sixteen years ago, when we saw *Mrs. Soffel* at the Paramount in New York. It was there that I first entertained the notion of falling hard for the six-foot-four-inch man with the lumberjack's beard and fifty-four-inch chest who would turn out to be my white knight. I still remember the exact moment it happened, as we rode the escalator down to the theater. "Do you cry at movies?" I asked. He pondered the question for a moment, then looked down at me thoughtfully. "Only the sad ones," he said.

We have since cried a river and laughed ourselves silly over mountains of popcorn in movie houses from coast to coast: huge cineplexes just off the highway, art cinemas in converted old barns, private screening rooms in the city, struggling drive-ins in the middle of nowhere. All told, we've seen a handful of truly great movies, dozens of good ones, and a fair number of bombs. But we approach every one of them as an adventure, a journey to some exotic new land. And each time the lights go out, we reach for each other's hand, in order to go there together. Cheaper than a vacation, more powerful than a rented video, able to refresh tired marriages in a single reel. That's the true magic of cinema, in this critic's opinion.

The next time the going gets rough, take your mate to a movie. Eat popcorn and Junior Mints and hold hands in the dark. Add an extra half hour at the end to relive your adventure over a glass of wine or a cup of espresso. Determine which characters you most identify with and what morals or lessons you take away. Invent your own private rating system using body parts other than thumbs, something that makes you both laugh. Discuss all the previews and decide what to see next. Keep holding hands as you head home together.

Here's looking at you, kids.

> Men would wither and custom stale them, but diamonds!
> Ah, they were crystallized immortality!

MAE WEST

WHEN LADY DI, not yet a princess, showed the world her engagement ring, a gigantic sapphire encircled by much smaller diamonds, I was terribly disappointed. She'd gotten the prince and the palace, after all. A sapphire instead of a diamond? It seemed a bad omen to me.

My grandmother was not born a princess, but her marriage was a real fairy tale. My grandfather died almost two decades ago, yet her love affair with him lingers on. At ninety-four her memory isn't what it was, but she can still recall every detail of the spring day in 1926 when my grandfather handed her the small Woolworth's box. It was, he said, all he could afford. It was only after she'd smiled and told him it didn't matter that he produced the real thing, one and a half carats in platinum. Would their love have en-

dured without it? Undoubtedly. But doesn't love like
that deserve its own shining star?

Except for the diamonds, I never bought into the
fairy tale. I waited until I was thirty-two to get married,
in a small wedding that was resolutely nontraditional. I
wore raspberry velvet and carried Queen Anne's lace.
The ceremony was brief and no-frills, though we did exchange matching gold rings. I was proud of myself and
my nonconformist husband as we cut into our wedding
cake: green apple, one layer, with fresh flowers on top.

Still, there were moments. When we'd announced
our intention to marry, a female relative had grabbed
my left hand and immediately started shrieking, "Let's
see!" There was no engagement ring, nor would there
be one. It made no sense at all, we'd agreed. But at that
precise moment, no price seemed too high. We had the
rest of our lives to be practical. Wasn't I worth one ex-
travagant gesture? I was ashamed of myself for caring.
How superficial. How trite. But undeniable. I wanted a
diamond—a big one—before I died.

Years passed. I got the house and the dog, though
not the children, sadly enough. I also became a secret
diamond junkie, addicted to brilliant white light. At
every wedding I went to, I checked out the rings. When
a younger cousin bought his fiancée an enormous diamond, one he'd be paying off for years to come, my
family was horrified. I was enthralled—and speechless
with jealousy.

My husband, of course, was well aware of my fixation. It became a joke every year when he asked what I wanted for my birthday: a diamond ring or a horse, my other girlhood obsession. I said it again several years ago, when he asked what I wanted for my upcoming fortieth. By his reaction, I figured I stood a better chance of getting the horse.

Still, I campaigned long and hard. I left my gold wedding ring on his dresser, lest he not know my size. I dropped terms like color, cut, and clarity into conversations about dry cleaning and car repair. I painted my nails fire-engine red for the first time in years. I was shameless. I just couldn't help it.

Then, a week before my birthday, I had an attack of fiscal restraint helped along by an ominous rattle in our ancient Honda. What was I thinking? A person needs food, water, shelter, transportation. A person does not need precious gems. I apologized to my husband for my recent behavior. I offered several gift options that were considerably more down-to-earth. My husband took the mail-order catalog I offered and tucked it into his briefcase. I silently kissed my shining star good-bye.

My birthday arrived. He made coffee, seated me at the table, then disappeared to get my presents. "Presents." That clinched it. I mean, think about it: nobody who was getting a diamond would be getting anything else. He'd taken my words at face value, done the sensible thing yet again. I felt relieved. I also wanted to weep.

Then he was back, empty-handed, a nervous look on his face. "I lied," he announced. "There's just one present." He reached into his pocket and produced it, the little blue box of my dreams.

With shaking hands, I opened it, saw the starlight inside, snapped it shut, burst into tears, threw my arms around his neck, and sobbed into his collar.

Finally! Forever.

**Money won't buy happiness,
but it will pay the salaries of a large
research staff to study the problem.**

BILL VAUGHAN

SOME SAY MONEY is the root of all evil, but I say it's Quicken, the program that enables you to organize your finances in neat rows of debits and credits stacked on top of each other. The very last number was the one that refused to crunch, not even in response to my threats, which grew more and more ominous the later it got. I briefly considered staying up a bit longer, but I could hear my bed calling my name. It turned out to be yet another mistake; my error came with me and insisted on spending the night. I imagined it as a pea sitting under my mattress while I flopped around on top, visions of overdrafts dancing in my head.

Meanwhile, my husband snored on beside me, as unconscious as someone in a Beautyrest ad. Far be it for him to lose sleep over money. Why should he worry, he says, when I obviously do it so well? He has a point. And yet, my tendency to fret about money has never stopped either one of us from spending it. In that sense we're two peas in a pod. We may not be well off, but at least we're compatible, nothing to sneeze at these days. More couples break up over money than any other single issue—not that money's a single issue, of course. It's more like an amalgam of every issue there is: our relationships with our parents. Our sense of self-worth. Our feelings of insecurity. Our thoughts on what the future may hold.

To tell the truth, I didn't begrudge him his slumber. Well, not entirely. While we tend to be in total agreement when it comes time to actually spend money, we often disagree about when is the right time. We can look at the bottom line and see two totally different scenarios. Whereas I see the need for immediate cutbacks, he sees a fortnight in Europe. I've long since realized that I need a much bigger cushion in order to sleep well at night, if only to accommodate the small crowd of relatives determined to share my mattress with me.

That night, my father came in first with his litany of Great Depression horror stories that are the Grimm's fairy tales of my generation. Next came my coupon-clipping mother, whose latest idea of the perfect gift to send me was a copy of *The Rookie's Guide to Money Management*. Joining us last was my thrifty grandmother, who I suspect keeps a box tucked away in her closet labeled String Too Short to Save. Is it any wonder I feel the need to rebel against all this financial austerity? Or that my ongoing rebellion is accompanied by massive quantities of good-daughter guilt? That a mere mathematical miscalculation should come to represent the pea under my mattress, the tiny irritant that robs me of sleep?

OK, so it wasn't so tiny; more the size of an apple or pear. The point is, it could have been a Dole pineapple and my husband wouldn't have felt a thing. Like so many couples, we have far different comfort levels with regard to how much is enough. The best we can do is to recognize this and be sensitive to our partners' needs, to acknowledge these worries and help assuage them, through communication, sound planning, and patience.

Despite his lack of financial anxiety, my husband has learned to help me deal with mine, although he knows better than to interfere when I'm busy beating myself to a pulp. And so he listened as I ranted and raved the next morning, sobbing about the mistake I had made. The front of his shirt soaking wet with my tears, his brow furrowed with loving concern, he simply patted my back consolingly and murmured "There, there" until I calmed down.

Then he asked me a question that reminded me how we stay married, even during the leanest of times: "Shall I assume that this error was not in our favor?"

Fond as we are of our loved ones,
there comes at times during their absence
an unexplained peace.

ANNE SHAW

W HAT ARE YOU up to this weekend?" I asked my
friend Janice, hoping we could take in a movie
or lunch. "Sorry," she said, with the hint of a smirk, the
Mona Lisa in T-shirt and jeans. "John's leaving for a
conference on Friday. He won't be back until Monday,
so . . ."

So, in other words, Girlfriend, dream on. I could
imagine her weekend already: crawling back into bed
with her first cup of coffee, eating mountains of popcorn at dusk, watching endless chick flicks with a
wadded-up hankie, crying her eyes out all night. My efforts to camouflage my envy were somewhat less con-
vincing than her efforts to cover up her glee.

Home alone. Are there any words in the language
more luxurious than these? More filled with the

promise of true self-indulgence? More mellow and soothing and sweet? Ask any woman who's been married awhile what the words *home alone* mean to her: a chance to revel in solitude, to relax and regroup. At least, that's the line of bull she'll serve up. If you press her, however, she may tell the truth: she won't be alone, not exactly; she'll be entertaining her friends, Ben and Jerry. Ernest and Julio may be dropping by later.

The studio that made *Home Alone* missed the boat, regardless of how much it earned. Instead of portraying a kid left behind while his family went on vacation, Hollywood should've told the tale of a middle-aged wife whose husband has left town on business. Forget *Body Heat, 9 1/2 Weeks,* or *Eyes Wide Shut. This* is the ultimate female fantasy.

It's not that we don't love our husbands or miss them when they go away. But the urge to indulge is a powerful one, as primal as any there is. No dessert tastes as rich, no bath lasts as long, as when there's nobody else in the house. Long, gossipy phone calls, a whole day in sweat pants, a fat stack of *People* or *Vogue.* A few guilty pleasures to savor in secret with nary a witness in sight. Not all the time, mind you. Just once in a while.

I've been known to crawl into bed well before nine o'clock on a cold, snowy evening in March, with a glass of wine, half a pound cake, and the remote control in my fist. My friend Claire holes up with her computer; my sister with a cheesy novel or two. I know of one woman who shall remain nameless whose idea of the perfect evening alone involves tweezers and a bag of Doritos (believe me, you don't want to know).

Whatever your solitary pleasure, feel free to indulge it—and yourself—to the hilt the next time your husband leaves home. Remember, you are part of a noble tradition, a secret sisterhood that exists just behind the drawn shades of every house where a wife is home alone.

Who needs a man for a romantic evening? All it takes is a loaf of bread, a jug of wine. And me.

Compromise is something people write about.
It does not work well in real life.

JUDY MARKEY

YOU ADORE CHOCOLATE. Your mate loves va-
nilla. You're a morning person; he's a night owl.
Your notion of the perfect way to spend Sunday morning is to read the papers and drink coffee till noon. His
idea of the ideal weekend morning is a five-mile run
through the park.

Compromise is the watchword of marriage; it's the
answer to conflict and strife. But what happens when
there is no ideal middle ground? When it's either/or,
yes or no, black or white?

When you want a dog and your mate says "No way."
When you want to move and he doesn't. It's not always
possible to meet him halfway, to accommodate both of
your needs. And while it may be feasible for you to take
turns, even that obviously doesn't work all the time.
There are always some issues that can't be resolved in a

way that will satisfy both. Somebody loses and some-body wins, and that's the way life tends to go.

So how do you cope when you can't have your way? That depends on the issue, of course. But learning to cope with or without certain things is essential to making love last. That may mean biding your time for a while and trying your best to adjust. When I wanted a baby and my husband did not, we tried counseling for a few months. He changed his mind, but my joy was short-lived: every pregnancy ended in miscarriage. We found ourselves once again facing a choice: whether or not to adopt. He voted no and I voted yes. There was no compromise to be had.

I decided to try living my life without kids, just to see if I could come to terms. It was painful at first, but in time I discovered a new door had opened for me. I ended up with a horse—not quite what I'd pictured, but a wonder-ful substitute nonetheless. In the end I was able to satisfy my need for a creature to nurture and love. I have no re-grets about how things worked out, even though I did not succeed in getting my way. That might not be true if I hadn't been open to all that I could have instead.

Flexibility, resilience, and openness are invaluable marital aids. When the answer isn't obvious, give it some time and wait and see what option lies ahead. It may look different from what you had in mind, but that isn't to say it can't work. Happiness comes in un-predictable ways; the key to finding it lies within you. Remember that the next time you believe you have lost. You may find you both win in the end.

Sharing is sometimes more demanding than giving.

MARY CATHERINE BATESON

MY HUSBAND IS shopping around for a sailboat, and I'm already wary—not of him, mind you. Of *her*. Oh, she'll be a pretty thing, sleek and graceful, and what is that sailor term that means seaworthy? *Yar*. She'll be yar, and I'll be jealous—jealous of an inanimate object.

The nerve! Not of him, mind you. Of me. For four years now, my husband has good-naturedly shared my affections—and countless hours of my leisure time— with another guy. An incredibly handsome other guy whom I'm constantly kissing and hugging. A guy for whom I sneak out of bed every morning to make break- fast. A guy with big, rippling muscles and even bigger vet bills. Of course, I could argue a gelding's no threat, but I'd only be kidding myself. Marriages can and do break up over less. Look around you: it happens a lot.

Love triangles come in all shapes and sizes, and

they don't always involve a third person. Consider a few of the myriad possibilities: a woman, a man, and a new Harley-Davidson. A couple and a fly fishing rod. All it takes is a passion both partners don't share: hang-gliding. Bird-watching. Football.

When I stopped trying to have a baby and acquired Eli, my horse, an old ache in my heart finally eased. At last I had someone to nurture and love, someone dependent on me. But horse ownership proved much more complex than that, richly marbled with conflicts and guilt. Unlike a baby, who would have been ours, Eli belongs only to me. My husband shares in the burden but not in the joy. While I've been off nurturing and learning to ride, he has gone without a great many things, not the least of them me.

There have been times when I sensed his resentment, even times when he made sure I did. But I can honestly say there haven't been many. There have also been the times when he shared in my pleasure, when he gave up his day to come watch. And when I went to the barn and walked into a nightmare, the day when my horse was so sick, he was the person I called in a panic. My husband, who knows nothing about horses but a great deal about me, heard my tone and said, "I'll be right there."

And so, I will too, when she goes into the water, the dream he has so long deferred. I'll be nervous and queasy and if the wind starts to gust, I'll be gripping her rails for dear life. But I'll be there. I only hope I will learn to share him with his love half as well as he shares me with mine.

**Honesty without compassion and understanding
is not honesty, but subtle hostility.**

R OUGHLY HOW MANY times a day do you lie to
your partner? Be honest. 'Fess up. Tell the truth.

The truth is, most of us would be very hard-pressed
to get through a whole day with no lies. I'm not talking
about vicious whoppers here, friends, I am speaking of
little white lies. They're a fact of life for virtually every
couple I know, and there's nothing the matter with
them.

If you disagree, take a moment to ponder the following often-asked questions:

"Does this make me look fat?"

"Is she prettier than me?"

"Did you think the white meat was too dry?"

Now consider the answers you're likely to give when
your partner starts questioning you:

"Another new dress?"

"Feel like fooling around?"

And, of course, "Does this make me look paunchy?"

Honest answers to questions like these could trigger some terrible fights, and for what? For grief we don't need, which is why we choose never to tell the truth in the first place. Better to fib than to hurt, we conclude, or to ruin the evening, or day. Which is fine— even admirable, in a way—provided we don't let it get out of hand. When we say we had one drink but we really had four, when "retail therapy" lands us deeply in debt, when "working late at the office" is merely an alibi for being where we shouldn't be, we are no longer protecting our partner's best interests. We're lying to safeguard our own.

There are two kinds of lies we can tell to our mates, one destructive, the other benign. And when it comes to the odds of confusing the two, there's no such thing as an honest mistake.

How do I love thee?

Let me count the ways.

ELIZABETH BARRETT BROWNING

MICHAEL AND KAREN are the Robert Browning and Elizabeth Barrett of our time, writing to each other three or four times a day, in what amounts to an ongoing chat. That they do this via e-mail in no way detracts from the content of their correspondence, an intimate exchange between husband and wife that takes place Monday through Friday without fail.

That isn't to say that their notes always reflect the passion they feel for each other. Some deal with carpools. Baseball games. Groceries. And yet, every now and then, wordplay becomes foreplay, and romance invades cyberspace. And by the time Michael gets home, they're both ready to explore the steamy side of married life.

As anyone who has seen *You've Got Mail* probably knows, e-mail can pack quite a punch, provided you don't accidentally send that X-rated note to your mother or colleagues or boss. A few hours apart can feel more like weeks when couples flirt electronically. All it takes are some well-chosen words to your mate between meetings or conference calls.

In the golden age of letter writing that ended a century ago, some cities delivered mail all day long. Thus, Barrett and Browning were able to "talk" via the mails, much the same as Karen and Mike. The relationship that inspired Barrett's "Sonnets From the Portuguese" began with a fan letter from Browning. There's nothing like scented paper, sealing wax, and script to spark some good old Victorian lust. But since few of us have time for that sort of thing anymore, a laptop is almost as good.

Half a letter a week is all most of us get, sandwiched between junk mail and the bills. Compare that with the four dozen letters Victor Hugo received on a typical day, or the sixty-five letters that awaited Edith Wharton upon her return from a three-day trip in 1924. Henry James's correspondence would have filled fifty volumes; in her lifetime, Virginia Woolf wrote twenty thousand letters.

Clearly, for them, all those letters were tools for honing skills and rehearsing their plots. But even those who didn't write for a living used letters to chronicle everyday life. And some of the most beautiful lines ever written were inspired by or rehearsed in love letters. Before it ever occurred to John Keats to write "A thing of beauty is a joy forever," he was writing passionate prose to Fanny Brawne: "Why may I not speak of your Beauty, since without that I could never have lov'd you?"

A far cry from "Stop at the store for some milk" or "Did you pay the MasterCard bill?" Still, between the reminders to pick up the kids, or the pizza, or drop off the shirts at the cleaners, there's still room for more intimate stuff. Think of it as a quick way to dash off a love letter of your own. And see if it doesn't inspire your mate to play "post office" when he gets home.

> **We commonly confuse closeness with sameness and view intimacy as the merging of two separate "I's" into one worldview.**
>
> HARRIET LERNER

THE SUN'S BARELY up as I write this; it is not even six o'clock yet. I am sitting at the picnic table behind Eli's barn, having woken up well before dawn. By the time my beloved reluctantly opens his eyes, I will have been very long gone. For a hard-core morning person such as myself, this is a beautiful thing.

It took me a long time to figure this out, but the truth of the matter is this: I am not missing much by leaving the house before dawn. In fact, I'm not missing a thing. My husband the night owl is not at his best in the hours before 10:00 A.M. After years of attempting to converse with him over coffee and bagels and juice, I have abandoned my fantasies of rising together in the interest of staying together.

Likewise, I'm no longer forcing myself to stay up

once my brain has shut down. I'm not much good past 10:00 P.M., so I usually just go to bed. Which is fine with my husband, since it's really no thrill to watch me struggle to stifle my yawns. And both of us seem to need time to ourselves at the opposite ends of the day.

I've been getting up with the chickens for roughly three years, and they've been three of the best years we've had. We've eliminated our "bad time" from each other's lives, and it's made a big difference to us. The phrase *quality time* may seem like a cliché, but it best describes the hours we share. Anytime between 10:00 A.M. and 10:00 P.M. seems to work fairly well for us both. We may spend it at the dining room table, reading the papers and drinking French roast; walking the beach with our big black Lab, Jake; building a fire and watching a film; or running errands and stopping for lunch. If you wake up happy and your partner does not, why not try to get up and get out? Start your day early—you'll be amazed at how much you'll get done while your partner's asleep. Steer clear during your "bad" time of day and you may even find you fight less. If you still miss the feeling of waking up side by side, try substituting a new ritual: call your mate at the office when he's wide awake and his grumpiness has disappeared. Meet him for coffee or lunch if you can, or send him an e-mail from work. The point is to stop trying to shoehorn yourselves into a model that just doesn't fit. There are twenty-four hours in every new day. Share the best. Spare each other the rest.

We challenge one another to be funnier and smarter. . . .
It's the way friends make love to each other.

ANNIE GOTTLIEB

CRAIG AND STEPHANIE Tyler are having dinner with the Marshalls on Saturday, their one bright spot in an otherwise dismal week. They planned it that way. Somehow it made them feel better to know they'd be ending it on a good note.

Mike and Laura Marshall are Craig and Stephanie's oldest friends. They met waiting in line for half-price theater tickets in Manhattan's Times Square, two young couples who'd just started dating. They struck up a conversation that continued until they got up to the ticket window, where they discovered the show they'd all wanted to see was sold out, so they wound up sharing a pizza instead. Fourteen years, three children, and countless pizzas later, they still go out together, though not as often as they'd like. The Marshalls live in New Jersey with their one-year-old; the Tylers in Connecticut with three-year-old twins. On the rare occasions when both couples manage to find sitters the same night, they meet in Manhattan, where their courtships—and their friendship—began.

Craig and Stephanie have plenty of friends who live a lot closer to home, but this friendship isn't about convenience. Laura and Mike are a link to their romantic beginnings, that time when their love was brand-new. When their biggest decision was whether to eat Chinese or Mexican. When their arguments were about politics and philosophy instead of housework and bills. When they spent more time in bed, almost none of it sleeping. Getting together with Laura and Mike, revisiting their old haunts, and reminiscing about the past helps both couples recapture the old magic and gives their marriages a shot in the arm. They find themselves flirting more and arguing less. The tension between them dissolves. Small wonder the Marshalls and Tylers jokingly describe these nights out as therapy, and each other as their marriage counselors. Neither couple intends to hang out a shingle, but they do volunteer this advice: When real life starts to threaten your romance, get together with a couple who knew you both when. Talk about old times, relax, and have fun. Turn back the clock and pretend you're still dating. Flirt shamelessly all the way home.

**I love it, I love it; and who shall dare
To chide me for loving that old armchair?**

ELIZA COOK

There's nothing wrong with sitting on the floor. My dog has been doing it for years. So has my husband—not because he isn't allowed on the furniture, but because for some time now, we haven't owned any furniture he cared to sit on. As seating goes, though, the floor has its drawbacks, which become increasingly obvious as we age. And so, when my husband suggested for the umpty-umpth time that we bite the bullet and buy some new chairs, I put on my coat, reached for my purse, and tried to look more optimistic than I felt.

It is a sad fact of married life that husbands and wives don't always see eye to eye on the best way to feather their nests. It's an ongoing debate and a common one, and it basically comes down to this: Women want style. Men demand comfort. And their demands escalate over time.

Take us, for example. In the early years of our relationship, when we were merging two households into one, my husband agreed to jettison his beloved Naugahyde recliner, a gesture symbolic of love. We replaced it with a camelback sofa; the first of many furnishings we would shop for together and the last we'd ever buy without a fight. It also happened to be the piece we were replacing when we entered the furniture store.

We parted ways at the door and got on with our mission: to sit in every chair in the place. Our plan was to meet in the middle and compare notes on what we had found. For the next twenty minutes, I wandered around like a dark-haired version of Goldilocks herself: This chair is too wide. This chair is too soft. This chair is too ugly for words.

And on and on, chair after chair, until I thought I had sat in them all. That's when I saw it, beckoning from the corner: a mission-style chair with wide cherry arms and firmly stuffed cushions. I sank into its depths and pressed my aching back against its firmness. Heaven. But wait! What was this? The chair seemed to be moving beneath me, bringing my shoulders back and my feet out in front of me, cradling my behind in a hammock of restful support. I closed my eyes and gave myself over to the feeling of comfort and bliss. I was still suspended there five minutes later, when I felt someone standing over me.

"We picked the same chair," my husband said with a grin. "A recliner, like the one I threw out." I looked up, aghast, realizing that he was right, that we'd grow old in our mission-style twin La-Z-Boys. The horror. The horror! Then again, what the heck. "I won't tell if you don't," I said.

The chairs were delivered a few weeks ago, and I'm curled up in mine as I write. I must say, I'm already quite fond of this chair and no longer embarrassed at all. Truth be told, I am actually quite pleased to have learned we find comfort in the very same thing.

And as it happens, a chair that becomes a recliner is a good metaphor for married life. It never hurts to be flexible and capable of change, especially the kind you never thought you could make.

Music is an incitement to love.

LATIN PROVERB

YOU MUST REMEMBER this: As nightclub owner Rick Blaine in the classic wartime film *Casablanca,* Humphrey Bogart portrays a man who sticks his neck out for no one. Cynical to a fault, Rick never allows himself to be affected by others' misfortunes, not even the shooting death of a patron inside the café. Rick's facade never crumbles—until his piano player takes a request for "As Time Goes By." The minute it reaches Rick's ears, he storms out from behind closed doors, his emotions unleashed at last. "Sam! I thought I told you never to play it!"

Such is the power music exerts over memory. And therein lies the reason all couples need songs. Just a few bars of "As Time Goes By" send Rick Blaine reeling all the way back to Paris, into the arms of his true love, Ilse Lund, just as the first bars of "Cherish" catapult me back to junior high school, and my first kiss from my first boyfriend, Steve. "It Had to Be You" enables Claire and Gerry to relive their wedding day whenever they feel like it. "Arthur's Theme" reminds Evan and Claudia of that long-ago day when their friendship caught fire and turned into love.

Some say it with flowers, but I like violins, saxophones, and pianos. Add a few candles, a soft summer breeze, and I turn to putty. As S. J. Perelman once said: "I tried to resist his overtures, but he plied me with symphonies, quartets, chamber music, and cantatas." And love songs. Especially love songs. I have never been so jealous in my life as when my friend Patricia told me how she and her fiancé, Steven, end the day: dancing cheek to cheek to Jimmy Durante singing "Make Someone Happy." Their song.

That's what convinced me it's never too late to set your relationship to music. (That and the blank look I got from my husband when I asked him to sing me *our* song.) So we're considering several possibilities, a fun exercise in itself. "Stardust." "Unchained Melody." "Misty." If you, too, are songless, sit down this week and compile your own list of contenders, to be whittled down to the top three or four. Go with the old standards, as opposed to this week's number one hit; like your love, your song should be here to stay. Play them and dance in the living room to determine which nominee suits you best. Make the occasion more memorable by planning a special dinner, perhaps adding candlelight and champagne. Dress up, if you care to, in something chiffon. Turn your mental clock back to the for-ties, that era of effortless grace. Think Cyd Charisse, Ginger Rogers. Think Gene Kelly. O'Connor. Astaire.

Once you've made your selection, take your act on the road. Put on your dancing shoes and visit a supper club, any place that has live music. Write your request on a cocktail napkin, and ask your waiter to deliver it for you. That way, when the first few bars of "Night and Day" reach your ears, you can both feign surprise as you head for the dance floor. Say, "Darling! They're playing our song."

Let there be spaces in your togetherness.

KAHLIL GIBRAN

KAHLIL GIBRAN MAY have said it more poeti-
cally, but I think my sister actually said it best:
"Are you insane?" she inquired, when I admitted to having dragged my husband to the big December crafts
show in a neighboring town a few years ago. She had a
point. She and I had always gone together to this an-
nual event, where we'd done the bulk of our Christmas
shopping in a joyous orgy of spending that had lasted
the better part of a day. We'd done this for years, right
up until she and her family moved to Los Angeles, leaving a huge, gaping hole in my life. But the mind is a
powerful thing. Mine wasted no time in plugging my
shopping-hating husband into the void, spinning
happy delusions of the two of us strolling arm in arm
through the mall. Oh, the fun we'd have hunting for
bargains and trying on clothes! I was very, very sick.

We lasted less than an hour at the crafts show, my

beloved and I, before walking out, empty-handed and seething. In icy silence we drove home, where I immediately called my sister to complain about having married a man who's no fun. "What were you thinking?" she asked. The same thing he was thinking when he dragged me on that marathon bike ride: that it was up to us as married people to fulfill each other's every need. "That's ridiculous," said my sister. "He may be the person you'd most want to be stuck with on an island, but you're not stuck on an island. Don't let your marriage become one."

I had done it without even thinking, as so many newlyweds do. When our relationships are brand-new, we all have the tendency to want to spend every moment together, the result of our insecurities as well as our love. Their hobbies become our hobbies, their preferences our preferences. Big sale at Bloomies? You betcha! A five-hour bike ride? Sounds great! It's only after the initial euphoria wears off that we start to reclaim our identities as people who hate shopping or bike rides. But by then it's too late. Rather than confess, we maintain the charade, our resentment growing with each store we visit and every mile we ride.

For Christmas that year, along with various other presents, my husband and I gave each other something priceless: the gift of space. I no longer feel guilty saying no to a bike ride. He doesn't feel obligated to go shopping with me. The truth is, there are plenty of people I'd rather shop with. And I'm not his first choice when he's looking for someone to accompany him on a ride. Having come to terms with this, we're both a lot happier. And the time we do spend together, we enjoy.

If your relationship is in danger of becoming an island, give yourselves permission to visit the mainland. Call up a friend you haven't seen in a while, and encourage your partner to do the same. Organize a ladies' night out or go see a "chick flick" with a girlfriend. Encourage him to play softball or poker with his pals. This week, spend a Saturday apart doing your own thing, then come home and do something together.

In other words, give your relationship a rest. It'll still be there when you get back.

Make just one someone happy.
And you will be happy too.

BETTY COMDEN, ADOLPH GREEN,
AND JULE STYNE

WHEN MY HUSBAND invited me to go sailing on Sunday, my first thought was: I can't possibly go. I had a staggering number of chores facing me, along with errands I'd put off all week. The cupboard was bare and the hamper was full. Why was he doing this to me? He knows Sunday's my day to get organized for the week and to spoil my animals a bit. But then I thought of all the times I'd said no to him lately; I couldn't remember the last time I'd said yes. So I sighed deeply and said, Sure, I'd love to. I'm not sure which one of us was more surprised.

He wanted to leave by eleven, which meant I'd need to rush through my daily ride on my horse in order to be back home by ten. Since it takes me two hours just to drive to the barn and back, that meant getting up before dawn. I was starting to wish I'd said no after all when my alarm woke me up at five-thirty. Most Sundays I spend extra time with my horse, as a thank-you for all his hard work. I give him a bath and let him dry in the sun while he eats grass and frisks me for treats. Instead, I rushed through our ride and a cursory grooming. Back in his stall, Eli turned away from me and sulked, just to let me know he knew the difference. So did I, and I felt like a heel. Back at home, my Lab, Jake, looked equally miffed as I raced past him to shower, only to walk out without him again.

The skies were sunny and clear and a south wind blew lightly as my husband and I drove away, but my dark mood persisted in spite of the weather. I envisioned Eli in his stall and felt guilty. I pictured Jake in the house and felt sad. My husband tried to make conversation as we drove to the dock, but my replies were perfunctory at best. I kept wishing I'd stayed at the barn a bit longer, or taken Jake for a swim at the lake. I glared at the back of my beloved's head as I followed him onto the boat. I sure hope you're happy, I thought.

But he wasn't, of course. He was too busy sneaking sideways glances at me, taking stock of my terrible mood. By the time we shoved off, he looked downright unhappy. My attitude was becoming infectious—not the way a charming giggle can be infectious; more like strep throat or the flu.

It dawned on me then what a mess I could make of this beautiful spring afternoon. I'd decided we'd spend it together, to give him the gift of my time. But instead of giving it freely, I'd gotten hung up on the sacrifices I had made. A gift given grudgingly isn't worth very much, regardless of how much it costs. All it does for the other person is make him feel bad. It makes him wish you hadn't bothered at all.

I knew then I had to let go of the guilt in order to salvage the day. I visualized dumping it overboard, then watching it sink like a stone. Try this sometime and maybe you, too, will see how easy it can be to change course. By the time we'd shut off the engine and hoisted the sails, I could feel myself lightening up. I made a conscious decision to have a good time, to give this present with no strings attached. I apologized to my husband and said I was glad I'd decided to come after all. And surrendered to the magic of riding the waves, on winds as soft and warm as a horse's breath.

> **Couples who cook together stay together.**
> **(Maybe because they can't decide**
> **who'll get the Cuisinart.)**
>
> ERICA JONG

WE'RE GOING OUT tonight to one of our favorite places, where the food's always terrific
and the atmosphere's great. There'll be no check at the
end of the evening, and best of all, we're allowed—no,
encouraged—to bring the dog.

Amy and Gordon's place isn't a restaurant, although it's a rare weekend that doesn't find them side
by side in their kitchen, whipping up some fabulous
feast and spoiling their various friends rotten. Now
that Jessie, their daughter, is a teenager, she's usually
right in there with them, sautéing the onions or chop-
ping the herbs. From soup to nuts—bouillabaisse Mar-
seilles to hazelnut meringue—the resulting meals earn
consistent four-star ratings from the neighborhood's
amateur critics. And so does this couple's marriage, a

rock-solid partnership forged during their college days in the seventies.

Indeed, they seem ideally suited, despite—or because of—their differences. Gordon's the risk taker, creative and adventurous, while Amy's the cautious, meticulous type. So it is in the kitchen, where she follows recipes with surgical precision and he invariably cooks by instinct. And so it is in their nine-to-five lives. Amy was recently named a vice president of the bank where she's worked twenty years. Gordon, on the other hand, has just completed a job change that's easily the biggest risk of his life: after two decades in advertising, he's now building houses. And while this has caused Amy no shortage of sleepless nights, she's a firm believer in her husband's creative talents, having seen them firsthand all these years. Wise woman that she is, Amy's also aware of the need to give her mate room to tinker around. In life, as in cooking, the best innovations often emerge from experiments, it seems.

Twenty-five years of cooking together have made them a very strong team. As Amy says, "The fact that we're all in the kitchen together makes me feel like I'm not the only one doing things for the family." She also appreciates the creative boost Gordon gives her, just as he marvels at her unfailing efficiency, bragging about her well-stocked pantry and the effortlessness with which she entertains.

Can bonds forged over hot stoves carry over to other aspects of everyday life? An interesting question, and one that might inspire us to rethink our divisions of labor, especially those of us who tend to be territorial, at least when it comes to our kitchens. "Need a hand with that?" asked my husband, as I chopped away at a huge pile of vegetables the other night. "No thanks, I'm fine," I said absently, automatically guarding my turf.

Next time I won't be so hasty. I'll invite him into my inner sanctum, to share the labor as well as the fruits. Why not attempt a similar joint venture in your own kitchen soon? Couples who cook together stay together, and not just because they want joint custody of the Cuisinart. They do it to strengthen their feelings of partnership. To work side by side as a team. To discover new ways to augment one another, the same way the spicy enhances the sweet.

buffer, *n.,* 1. **Something that lessens or absorbs the shock of an impact.** 2. **One that protects by intercepting or moderating adverse pressures or influences.** 3. **Something that interposes between two rival powers, lessening the danger of conflict.**

THE AMERICAN HERITAGE DICTIONARY OF
THE ENGLISH LANGUAGE

TECHNICALLY SPEAKING, our dog is a Labrador retriever, but practically speaking, he's much more than that. He's a surrogate child, companion, protector, fitness trainer, playmate, and friend. Whether he's running around with a toy in his mouth, egging us on to give chase; trotting obediently along on his leash; or just happily sprawled at our side, he also serves as a buffer between his two masters, constantly absorbing and deflecting, intercepting and reducing, the pressures of everyday life.

The presence of somebody else in the house is a

wonderful thing, I'm convinced. Especially someone as joyful as Jake, though I admit I am partial to dogs. Many's the morning he's made us both laugh, even before we've put coffee on. And many's the evening I've opened the door to send him bounding outside to greet "Dad"—to soften him up before he comes inside, to take the edge off a less-than-great day.

Couples need buffers, though they needn't be dogs. They can have fur, scales, or blue jeans, as long as they live on the premises, are reasonably responsive, and are capable of displaying affection. Babies and toddlers make excellent buffers, provided you have the right kind, the ones who smile and gurgle and sleep through the night. The other kind just make more stress. Unfortunately, both kinds grow up to be teenagers, often the very worst buffers of all.

Dogs, on the other hand, have some sort of genius for making their owners connect. Many's the night we've sat apart on the couch watching TV or reading our books only to have Jake leap between us and pull us together to rub his belly, pat his head, scratch his ears. In the interest of harmony, stress management, and joy, I heartily recommend pets: fun-loving and loyal, entertaining and adoring, affectionate and mercifully incapable of talking back. Amiable escorts on the journey through life, selfless shock absorbers over the bumps.

But, soft! what light through yonder window breaks?
It is the east, and Juliet is the sun!

SHAKESPEARE

CTUALLY, IT WAS the west, and her name was
Fiona, but like most lost men, Romeo would
sooner wander aimlessly around Verona and woo the
wrong maiden than ask directions at a 7-Eleven.

I have been known to stop at a 7-Eleven, a Texaco
station, and a fast-food joint—all within a five-mile ra-
dius—and *still* wind up on the wrong interstate, but
that's another story. The point is, at no time have I considered my inability to get from point A to point B to be
anything other than a damn nuisance. But then again,
I'm not a guy.

The Lost Man phenomenon has been well docu-
mented by annoyed women passengers everywhere:
women in desperate need of a powder room, women in
danger of missing the big moment at their boss's surprise party, women entrusted to bring the hors d'oeu-

vres to dinner parties that started an hour ago. Women whose pleas have long since turned to threats falling on the deaf ears of the Lost Man beside them, who's driving in circles while loudly insisting he knows just where he is.

Lost Men—and you know who you are—will go to remarkable lengths to avoid asking directions, as my husband once proved in a thrilling demonstration that took place during the evening rush hour in the French city of Lyons, a place neither one of us had ever laid eyes on. *His* job was to circle the city with mounting impatience at sixty miles an hour, yelling the names of the streets as we blew past them. *My* job was to instantaneously locate these streets on a map half the size of the city, ascertain our location, and calculate the optimum route to our hotel. We've been back from Lyons thirteen years now. We're still fighting about it.

To be fair, I should add that Lyons was a fluke. My husband rarely gets lost, even in strange cities. Even without a map. I get lost *with* the map. But I'm not ashamed to admit it and ask for help, except, of course, when I find myself asking the same guy who drew me the map a half hour ago.

Here's the bottom line: don't expect a Lost Man to stop for directions. Make it a habit to get them yourself, *before* the two of you get in the car. Then casually mention that you'd been curious as to the best route to the restaurant and had been told to take exit 14 and turn left. And then—here comes the hard part—simply leave it at that. Do not mention the time you arrived forty minutes late for your eight o'clock reservation and didn't get seated until ten. Do not bring up the fact that by that time they'd run out of the duck.

Your Lost Man's ego will be spared. And so—praise the Lord—will your bladder.

Memory is more indelible than ink.

ANITA LOOS

I WAS CLEANING OUT my junk drawer the other day when I came across a small artifact: a gaudy red plastic heart that was stuck in a flower arrangement I received one distant Valentine's Day. It was my first with the man I would marry; he was out of town for the big day. I recall slouching at my desk at the office, moping that he wasn't around at the precise moment the flowers arrived. Well. That moment came back as I looked at that heart, and I suddenly wondered why it wasn't wrapped in wads of tissue paper and locked away in the vault at the bank.

What kind of saver are you? Do you save your kids' valentines? Or just their report cards and tests? Do you still have your dog's baby teeth? That ruffled nightmare you wore to your prom?

Given all the stuff we hang on to, the souvenirs of infancy, adolescence, past loves, and past lives, it's amazing how little we set aside for safekeeping from the relationship that matters the most. Oh, sure, we all stumble upon bits and pieces of our histories while hunting for extra batteries or cleaning out drawers. We'll be pawing away through the rubble in search of airmail stamps or a Phillips screwdriver, when suddenly, there it is: the hotel receipt from your honeymoon. A broken swizzle stick from your first date. Tiny relics, each one a small souvenir from your story, all scattered and broken and lost.

Today let's decide that these tokens have worth, and let's take steps to safeguard the past. We can start with a box, the bigger the better. A wooden blanket chest is ideal, although those cardboard wardrobe boxes that slide under the bed for storage are fine, too. This is your marriage box. It's empty at the moment, but you need only comb your closets, empty your drawers, search your files, and scour your basement for remembrances and mementos to fill it. That wishbone you saved from your first Thanksgiving together. Those dance trophies from your disco days. The first present he ever bought you, the black silk teddy you can no longer get past your hips.

If you can't put your hands on your keepsakes, don't worry. These are the sorts of things you find when you're looking for something else. The idea is to *start* the project today, not to finish it, since ideally you'll never be finished. Instead, you'll keep putting new items into the box: those matches from the four-star restaurant he took you to for your tenth anniversary. The velvet box containing the diamond earrings he gave you for Christmas. Be selective. Think of yourself as the curator and the box as a marriage museum.

And not just a museum, a mental makeover, for those days when the good times seem too far away. When you can't remember the last time the two of you had fun together. When you're convinced he never bought you anything that wasn't an appliance or took you to dinner anyplace that doesn't serve fries. That's when you'll poke through your marriage box and decide to stay married.

I'm starting mine now, before I lose one more priceless piece of plastic, one more odd artifact of our love.

They buried the hatchet,

but in a shallow, well-marked grave.

DOROTHY WALWORTH

SHORTLY AFTER GIVING birth to her first child, a son, my sister sent her husband on a mission of mercy, to go find her something to eat. He returned with a rare roast beef sandwich, blood red and dripping with "jus." Famished as she was, there was simply no way; she couldn't bear to even look at the thing. But instead of indulging her and bringing her something else, the proud papa threw a big hissy fit. Here he'd brought her a snack and she'd refused to go near it! What the hell was the matter with her?

The "baby" in question is now five feet nine, and I'm *still* hearing about the damn sandwich. My sister brought it up just this morning, no less furious than she was at the time. Fourteen years have gone by since her husband screwed up; it's clearly time to forgive and forget. But for reasons that defy reason, she can't let it go. Her anger simmers on just under the surface, ready to leach into her marriage at all times.

The sandwich fiasco is a perfect example of what I think of as marital waste, the by-products of old fights and past petty grievances that were never completely resolved. I have some, too, cooking up noxious fumes in my landfill of dastardly deeds: the wedding at which my then-boyfriend kept dancing and flirting with somebody else; our wedding rehearsal dinner, at which he ignored me completely, spending the whole time with visiting friends. I could go on but I won't, because that's not the point of the ritual I've planned for today. Instead of steeping in my own bitter "jus" from the past, I am going to let it all go, to forgive every one of my husband's mistakes, to empty my toxic waste dump.

Since burying it hasn't done the trick yet, I am planning to burn it instead. I will write each crime down on a separate slip, then feed them, one by one, to the flames. This being summer, I'm using the grill, but a fireplace would work just as well.

Why not join me in burning your own noxious stuff, the old resentments that poison your love? Invite your husband to attend the ceremony as well, to let go of his old grudges, too: the time you embarrassed him in front of his boss. The day you threw away his lucky socks.

As the sparks rise up phoenixlike over your heads, you can celebrate starting anew. Once the coals turn a nice, ashy gray, why not throw a piece of top round on the grill? Cook it medium rare and slice thinly for sandwiches like the one my sister refused to choke down. I'm hoping she'll try again one of these days, before her son has a son of his own.

My God,
who wouldn't want a wife?

JUDY STYFERS

M Y FRIEND AMY is an events planner. Barbara is a travel agent. Linda's a social director, and Margaret's a chef. And I? I'm every one of those things and then some—not because I have any special talent for them or because I love doing them all, but simply because I'm a wife.

Where is it written that women must book all vacations, schedule get-togethers with friends, arrange dinner parties, and plan holiday outings? Who says it must fall to the woman to facilitate friendships, engineer social events, and buy presents for every last relative—including the ones on his side? I'd like to know, because I want to talk to him. That's right, him. Because whoever it was who decreed this is so, you can bet your boots he was a man, a man who turned to his wife two or three times a year and asked where they'd be spending July.

One who wanted to know what the plans were for Christmas . . . whom they'd be dining with Saturday night . . . when they'd be throwing their next party . . . what she was planning to serve.

Naturally, women are partly to blame. For planning vacations, nurturing friendships, giving parties, and buying the gifts. For making sure that these things all get done and done well, and to our precise specifications. No matter how busy we are, and no matter how badly we don't want to do them at all.

How many Saturday nights would we need to stay home before our partners picked up the dropped ball? How many vacations would go by the boards? How many holidays would we spend all alone? My friend Cindy, fed up with her mate's expectations, decided to try it and see. After three barren months, Richard figured it out. They're flying to Aruba next week for a holiday planned by Himself, without any help whatsoever from her. Cindy's ecstatic—and who wouldn't be? She's getting what every wife wants: a respite from the burden of her husband's good time. And all it took was a ninety-day strike.

Once they get there, of course, she will need to be pleased, no matter how badly things go. No matter how big a dump their hotel turns out to be, no matter how disappointing their meals. No matter how differently she would have done things. Because he won't be willing to take charge again if she bad-mouths the choices he's made. Let that be a lesson to each one of us who has had it with doing it all. Letting someone else do things means losing control of the manner in which things get done. While that may not be easy, it's still worth a try for the chance to unburden ourselves. Chances are, he'll get better at doing these things, just as we will at letting him do them.

In a false quarrel,

there is no true valour.

SHAKESPEARE

BRADLEY AND KAREN are having a fight; sad to say, it is not even theirs. They are actually having Tommy and Jacqueline's fight, and here's the truly pathetic part: Tommy and Jackie have made up already. Yet Bradley and Karen fight on.

It started on Sunday when Karen and Jackie talked on the phone for close to an hour and a half. Jackie filled Karen in on the details of the fight she and Tommy had just finished up. Like any true friend, Karen took her friend's side; she felt her pain—to the point where she wanted to share it with Brad, which she did when she hung up the phone. And, like any true friend, Bradley took his friend's side, so instead of one fight, there were two.

As dumb as this is, I can truly relate, having been there with my husband, too. We don't always split along gender lines, though; he automatically sides with whomever I blame. I attribute this to the fact that my husband's a Libra, the sign of the balancing scales. However I lean, he will tip the other way, to maintain equilibrium at all costs.

The only solution I know is to refrain from discussing the fights that our closest friends have. This sounds simple, though sometimes it's anything but, given how easily friends suck you in. And no one I know likes to turn a deaf ear to a friend who is mad at her mate. Should you find yourself getting an earful from someone whose partner has just done her wrong, simply pick up the phone and call somebody else—anyone of the same sex. She will agree with you, and all will be well (until your friend's husband tells his side to yours).

Though it is fairly easy to describe what constitutes a bad home, there is no single definition of a good one. Conformity with the traditional pattern certainly is no guarantee of the happiest results.

ALVA MYRDAL AND VIOLA KLEIN

MY FRIEND AND I meet at the park at midday, to trade recipes, household hints, and domestic complaints while our dogs socialize, romp, and play. While we consider ourselves happily married, for the most part, we have a number of pet peeves in common, most having to do with not being appreciated for all we do around the house. Neither of us likes it when our spouses kick off their shoes and leave them lying around. Nor are we happy when we slave over a hot stove for a dinner our mates barely touch. Typical girl talk, except for the fact that my dog-walking pal is a guy. A guy with a talent for stir-fries and stews, but a red-blooded guy nonetheless.

Every Day I Love You More

Arthur and Laura have one of the more nontraditional marriages around. While she pursues her career with ambition and zeal, Arthur shops, mops, and cares for their "kid." Our dogs make quite a pair, a black Lab and a pug, as they traipse around Cranbury Park. As do Arthur and I, as we trail in their wake, venting frustrations and exchanging ideas. It was Arthur who taught me the best way to cook veal, clean my sink, and get rid of mildew. As incongruous as it seems to hear household hints spill from the lips of a guy from the Bronx with a five o'clock shadow that appears at high noon and an accent he's never quite lost, I have come to respect his perspective on marriage along with his domestic skills.

Having married a woman much younger than he, Arthur understands his mate's drive. He once had it, too, and pursued his photography career with a single-mindedness similar to hers. At forty-seven he's no longer as driven to make his mark on the workaday world. But having been there already, he cheers his wife on as she struggles to be a success. He, on the other hand, tries to squeeze in his photography assignments amid myriad errands and chores.

I don't know many men whose egos allow them to cede the career to their wives. Nine times out of ten, it's the women who sacrifice their ambition to cheer on their mates. They're the ones who stay home till the kids are in school, or who juggle their families, households, and jobs. As Gloria Steinem once said, "I have yet

to hear a man ask for advice on how to combine marriage and a career." Are you one of the jugglers who
struggle to keep several balls in the air all the time? If
so, you might try tossing one to your partner to take
some of the heat off yourself. You also might try spending some time with guy friends, since their perspective
can be eye-opening. It can also help you make sense of
your guy, thereby strengthening your relationship with
him.

Arthur and I often talk about such things on our
weekday walks around the park. I encourage his efforts
on Laura's behalf and enthusiastically applaud the results. As a female, I know how hard juggling can be.
And I suspect for a man it's more difficult yet to walk a
mile in a woman's shoes, teetering on heels that sink
into the ground from the burden of doing it all.

Happiness is a thing to be practiced, like the violin.

JOHN LUBBOCK

MY HUSBAND AND I went for a sail Friday night, and as I watched him scamper over the rigging, hoist the sails, and maneuver us into Long Island Sound, I saw the tension of the previous workweek slowly disappear from his face. Gone were the tiny lines between his eyes and the stiffness around his jaw, the tired slog of the breadwinner en route to the office at dawn. He looked totally different from the way he had looked as he shouldered his duties all week. For the first time in days, he looked like the person I married; he looked happy, in other words.

It occurred to me then as he fiddled and fussed, straightening lines and adjusting the jib, just how long it had been since I'd seen him like this, intent on play rather than work. Instead, I had seen him struggle to wake up in the morning, his eyes half shut and encrusted with sleep, or hunched over his computer, his brow furrowed with deep concentration. I'd seen him trudge to his car, weighted down with his briefcase and too much responsibility for one man. And I'd seen him return more than twelve hours later, looking depleted and beat.

How often do we get to see our mates happy, engrossed in the thing they love best? To watch the burdens of their daily lives slip away? To see weariness turn into joy? If your life is like mine, chances are, not enough. We're too busy with chores of our own.

Mine nearly kept me from going along, but something made me change my mind. Maybe I needed to see him like this, at least for an hour or two. To be reminded of how young he looks to me still, when the stresses of life are removed; how little he's changed in the years since we met; how quickly the time slips away.

Whatever your love loves to do most of all, take some time out this week to go, too. Hop on your bicycles, hike through the woods, swing a golf club, a racquet, a bat. Sail away from the burdens of everyday life, and you'll find him there, waiting for you—stripped of his worries and freed from his chores, looking much like he did when you met.

**Whoever thinks marriage is a fifty-fifty proposition
doesn't know the half of it.**

FRANKLIN P. JONES

MARRIAGE IS A partnership in which domestic chores are split right down the middle. Fifty-fifty. Even-Steven. Show me a person who's been married a while who sincerely believes this is true, and I'll show you a person who's not doing his half. In other words, I'll show you a man.

The notion of fifty-fifty is one of the most beloved and enduring myths about marriage that our curious culture has spawned. It is, of course, utter flapdoodle. And yet it lives on, despite mounting evidence to the contrary, evidence quietly being amassed by almost every married woman I know.

The equal division of labor as practiced by most modern couples these days tends to look something like this: *She* buys the groceries, cooks the meals, washes dishes, does the laundry, manages child care, pays the bills, and cleans the house (or hires someone to do it). All this in addition to her so-called real job. *He* mows the lawn, takes out the garbage, cleans out the rain gutters once a year, dissolves the occasional clog in the pipes, and tackles the routine repairs, provided she nags him enough.

That isn't to say that the typical husband isn't willing to lend you a hand. But that's generally how he perceives what he's doing: he's "helping" you out with "your" chores, meaning you'll still need to supervise him as he tackles the laundry, or your new sweater may end up fitting Barbie. While he may be happy to go to the market, he'll still need you to make him a list. And how many husbands are capable of finding someone (besides their mothers) to babysit on a Saturday night?

I'm not saying all this to depress you or to discourage you from your ongoing efforts to achieve a more equitable balance. All I'm saying is that as a rule, equal partnerships do not exist. At any given time, one person is typically doing the bulk of the work. There may be times now and then when that person's not you. But, half the time? Not even close.

In a perfect world, it's a wonderful concept. But in the real world, fifty-fifty's a joke. Measuring your respective contributions against a standard that doesn't exist only leads to resentment, and worse. Blame it on sex roles. Blame society. Blame his mother—and yours— if you wish. Get good and mad, then get over it. After all, as a wise woman named Marni Jackson once said, "Housework hassles go on, are never resolved, and will probably extend into the afterlife (Why am I the one who takes the clouds to the dry cleaners?)."

O, beware, my lord, of jealousy;
It is the green-ey'd monster which doth mock
The meat it feeds on.

SHAKESPEARE

J EALOUSY, THE "green-eyed monster," as Shakespeare dubbed it more than four centuries ago, is a fact of life in most relationships, from the sibling rivalry we experience as children to the love triangles that threaten our adolescent crushes. Few of us make the journey to adulthood without experiencing our fair share of its angst.

Few marriages escape it entirely, either, and while its causes and manifestations may appear less obvious to us as we age and mature, there's no mistaking the damage it does. When it's allowed to run amok in our lives, it can insidiously poison us all from within. At its worst, jealousy can trigger the sort of passionate crimes that land people in prison for life. But even low-level jealousy can destroy a marriage, by mutating love into hate. And it doesn't necessarily require a third party to effectively poison the well. For the most part, it takes only two: one to succeed and the other to fail, or even succeed to a lesser degree. Our relationships with our spouses are fluid shape-shifters worthy of the best science fiction. Sometimes we're siblings; sometimes we're friends. Sometimes we're parent and child. And in each of these pairings, jealousy plays a role that rekindles our earliest fears: the fear of abandonment, failure, or loss. Fear of losing the person we love. None of these fears go away as we age; they stay with us throughout our lives. But we don't always see them for what they are; we prefer to deny they exist. So we transform them into anger, resentment, even hate—whatever feels more acceptable to us.

When your partner's promoted to a high-profile job, when he achieves something worthy of note, when he loses forty pounds or makes a new friend, when your children love him more than you, when he beats you at your own game, the one you play best—in short, anything that threatens your view of yourself can awaken the monster in you.

You can't deal with these feelings until you face up to the fact that you have them at all, which in turn can add shame and remorse to the stew that is bubbling up inside you. When you know you should be delighted for your partner but you're also convinced that you're not, ask yourself if you're jealous, and try not to beat yourself up if the answer is yes. Admit it, discuss it, and know in your heart that it is something everyone feels. Once it's out in the open, you have a far better chance of overcoming it before it does harm. And when the shoe's on the other foot and your mate envies you, you'll be able to recognize that, too. Know it when you see it, and you'll stand a far better chance of getting rid of it before it hurts you.

**The guy who used to appear at your front door
every night because he was wild to see you,
now appears there every night because
that's where he happens to live.**

LUCILLE KALLEN

SOME NIGHTS ARE special and some nights are
not, and anyone who's been married for more than
a month would benefit from knowing the difference.
Take last night, for example, when my husband came
home looking weary and worn out from work. His expression awakened the cheerleader in me; I got perky,
and he got annoyed. Then I got hurt and he got more
annoyed. Then I wised up and left him alone.

There is no faster way to wear somebody out than
to treat every night like a date, to expect—or demand—a
good time all the time. To expect to connect on a level
that's deep. There are times when we all want to be left
alone, and there's nothing the matter with that. Putting
pressure on your partner night after night is exhaust-

ing for both you and him. Whereas learning to live with the fact that you won't click every day is an essential aspect of sharing your lives.

Most of the time I can spot these downtimes the minute my husband comes home. Now and then they slip by me and I find myself waving my pom-poms around in his face. Occasionally I turn a dull evening around, but that's more the exception than the rule. More often, I nudge us both into a bad mood that persists for the rest of the night.

Having done it again just last night, I've resolved not to try quite so hard the next time. Marriage is all about reading the signs and responding appropriately. The better we are at perceiving these cues, the more harmonious life tends to be. Living with somebody else doesn't alter the fact that we all want to be left alone. Not all the time, of course, only sometimes. And we count on our partners to understand.

The next time your partner comes home looking weary and greets you with a one-syllable word, take the hint and back off. Don't assume something's wrong, because chances are good that nothing is. Like Garbo, he just "vants" to be alone.

Although man has learned through evolution

to walk in an upright position,

his eyes still swing from limb to limb.

MARGARET SCHOOLEY

WE WERE ON our way to a dinner party in the neighborhood the other night when we drove past a jogger at dusk. She was wearing a tank top, short shorts, and a smile, and I knew what to expect right away. Sure enough, my husband's eyes made a beeline for the rearview mirror, and he gave her an obvious look. "Can I help you?" I asked, my hands balled into fists. "No thanks. Just looking," he said.

Let me say that I'm not so much threatened by this as I am offended, annoyed, and grossed out. As are most of the women I'm friends with whose husbands participate in this spectator sport. Nonetheless, over dinner with the girls a few nights later, it took several glasses of wine before the bulk of us finally came clean.

First we hemmed and we hawed and we argued a while, conflicted about how we should feel.

A few friends insisted their husbands don't look, which brought a chorus of "You wanna bet?" Maggie claimed she frequently points out well-endowed women when she and her husband go to the beach. "I don't have a problem with him looking at all," she informed us as she sipped her first drink. I have done the same thing on occasion, so I saw through my pal right away. A preemptive strike is less hurtful, after all, than watching him gawk on his own. By giving him permission, or even telling him to look, Maggie's hoping to lessen the sting.

We were mulling her strategy over in our minds when Kathleen finally piped up: "Looking at somebody else in my presence is really an affront to me." The rest of us nodded in agreement at that, the ice having been broken at last. "It's not really cheating exactly," said Claire, and we had to agree with that, too. But it does make us feel bad when the person we love clearly lusts after somebody else.

If they did it more subtly, we could pretend it didn't happen or dismiss it more easily. But swiveling heads, open mouths, and bug eyes are a little too much to ignore. Most men will still look no matter what their wives say; their brains are hardwired that way. But that's not to say we shouldn't raise the issue, especially if their ogling upsets us. Blatant hostility probably won't help, so try not to label your soul mate a pig. Try not to mention pork products at all. (If you can't stop yourself, I understand.)

And try not to ask the impossible. As I say, most are still going to look. What we can do is ask them to show some restraint when they're gawking in front of us wives. Don't swerve over the centerline, for example, or veer off onto somebody's lawn. Don't show us the back of your head for so long, or slow the car down to a crawl. If we want to pretend that you're one of the few who don't look at other women that way, try not to ruin it for us.

All things considered, in the grand scheme of life, we don't think that is asking too much.

**I love being married. It's so great
to find the one special person you want
to annoy for the rest of your life.**

RITA RUDNER

G REG AND CLARA, my neighbors, are having a
fight. Clara's not even up yet, so I don't know
which fight they're having, the one about money or the
one about work, but either way, I smell trouble. Actually, I
don't so much smell it as see it: their newspaper is still lying at the end of their driveway. That means Greg's gone
off to work without having first tossed the paper on the
porch for his wife, a small act of kindness he performs
every morning—*except* when they're having a fight. A little
thing? Maybe. But then again, maybe not, at least not in
January, when Clara's standing there barefoot and her
driveway is glare ice.

Like dogs, human couples have hidden lives filled
with symbols and gestures that are deeply personal,
highly significant, and usually meaningless to the rest

of us—which is, naturally, the whole point. Couples need secrets: they reinforce "two-ness." These secrets can take many forms: private pet names. Inside jokes. Passing references to past experiences. And, of course, the little red flag one partner waves at another to signify the start of a fight. These, too, vary widely. One couple's untossed newspaper is another's unlowered toilet seat, unemptied trash can, or unscoured pot. But while the medium may vary from marriage to marriage, the message behind it does not: Just in case you haven't noticed, I happen to be mad as hell.

Clara, of course, knows this. After twelve years of marriage, the mere sight of a newspaper at the end of her driveway prompts her to call Greg and ask him what's wrong. Nine times out of ten, she can head off a fight with that phone call, a call she might otherwise not have made, since her husband finds it difficult to express anger directly. Thus the newspaper serves as a sort of emotional shorthand the two of them find very helpful.

The next time you and your mate have a fight, pay attention to your actions as well as your words. What subtle—or not-so-subtle—messages lurk in your rituals of everyday life: the empty coffee pot, the dirty dish, the toothpaste tube squeezed in the middle? Learn to interpret these warning signals and defuse things at once, before your anger gets too out of hand.

Identify your secret language and build on it, adding pet names, inside jokes, and silly expressions that are good for a laugh when you need one. And you will.

When you care enough to send the very best.

HALLMARK CARDS ADVERTISEMENT

SOME FOLKS CRY at movies. I cry at cards. I'm talking Hallmark here, friends, not gin rummy. I thought I was alone with this peculiar affliction until I met Janice—and then there were two. Most women I know compare presents on Christmas, anniversaries, or Valentine's Day. But Janice and I never waste time discussing new jewelry or flowers or clothes. We're too busy putting our cards on the table, the better to share a good cry.

Our significant others have learned to shop wisely, for the right card can carry the day. It's a lesson my spouse learned the hard way, after coming cardless to our anniversary, an anniversary that shall live in infamy. When he realized the magnitude of his mistake, he rushed off to the store the next day. Since late cards don't cut it, the damage was done. I forgave him, but not right away.

But there have been great highs as well as great lows. The best card of my life also came from my husband.

It's a photo of a couple side by side, holding hands, but you see them only from midriff to knees. He's wearing denim overalls. She's twice his width in a faded blue housedress topped with a gingham check apron. They look tender and awkward, and by the looks of their hands, they are probably both pushing ninety. "I will always love you," it says.

I've received countless cards over the course of my marriage, but none that's affected me so, for that card holds the promise of a love that endures after beauty and youth fade away. The card endures, too. More than a decade ago, I wedged it into the mirror on my dresser where I can't help but see the old couple each day, the perfect antidote to my fears about aging. In fact, the card itself is slowly aging along with me, fraying a bit at the edges from the countless times I've handled it over the years.

In an age when we never need be out of touch, the more access we have to each other, the less thoughtful our notes seem to be, if we bother to write them at all. Instead, we produce corporate memos. We dash off electronic mail. We leave voice messages on our cellular phones. And when it finally comes time to speak from the heart, we can't seem to access the words.

But someone has already written them down, in a way that will jump-start your heart. So join Janice and me as we wander the aisles in search of cards that bring tears to our eyes. Try a little tenderness when your mate least expects it, and see what a great card can do. Cheap sentiment? Absolutely. Yet priceless, somehow, all the same.

A happy marriage is
the union of two forgivers.

RUTH BELL GRAHAM

RAVEN HAIRED, blue eyed, and fun loving, Steve
and Sandy look as if they were cut from the same
bolt of cloth. But appearances can be deceiving, at least
when it comes to their styles. Sandy is efficient and me-
thodical, the type who makes sure she has all her ducks
in a row before starting a task. Steve's hopelessly scattered and disorganized, the sort who makes seventeen
trips up and down the stairs by the time he finally com-
pletes a task. It's an old story and a common one: order
meets chaos; sparks fly.

But what happens after the wedding, when Order
and Chaos set up housekeeping together? That, too, is a
familiar old story: I love you. You're perfect. Now
change. With customary efficiency, Sandy immediately
set about the task of reforming her mate. Given her excellent example, she figured it would be a snap to trans-

form her absentminded other half into a paragon of precision.

All told, it took twenty-odd years, and in the end, it was Sandy who changed. Take last Tuesday morning, for instance: a typical morning in that, once again, Steve had lost his keys. As he ran around searching, Sandy poured herself a second cup of coffee and demonstrated just how far she has come. The old Sandy would have joined in the search, becoming more agitated with each passing moment. She'd have asked lots of questions that could not be answered: "When did you have them last?" "Where did you put them?" "Why can't you just leave them by the door?" And by the time they'd turned up, she'd have been stressed-out and frustrated, and most likely late for her job. And unlike Steve, who'd have gone off to work happily jingling his keys, Sandy would have carried that stress around with her, letting it color the rest of her day.

Compare that with the new Sandy, who sits at the table sipping coffee while her husband tears through the house. Rather than join in the search, she simply watches it, detached and amused as opposed to annoyed and uptight. Having accepted the fact that her husband will never change, she is free to enjoy the spectacle that is Steve in the morning. She's even able to tease him about his haphazard approach to life—and he's able to give it right back. These days when Steve misplaces his belongings, he accuses Sandy of having hidden them for the sheer joy of watching him search.

Their children, twenty-two-year-old Adam and twenty-year-old Aaron, join in the ribbing, and "we all start the day laughing instead of arguing," Sandy says.

It may sound simple enough, but Sandy's transformation was anything but. "As women, we tend to be caretakers," she says, "and that often means taking on everyone else's problems. Once we've taken them on, we have trouble letting go. If Steve minded the fact that he loses things, he'd find a way to become better organized. But it's never bothered him. I was the one who minded; therefore, I was the one with the problem."

I suspect there are few of us who can't relate, who can't learn from Sandy's example. As women, we're just so darned helpful—often at our own expense. If we weren't quite so quick to come to the rescue, we could save ourselves a great deal of stress. And who knows? We might even encourage our partners to take more responsibility for themselves. To be less dependent on us to look after them. To set a better example for our kids.

At any rate, who wouldn't rather start the day off with a good laugh instead of a squabble? The next time my husband misplaces his keys or forgets what he did with his wallet, I'm planning to pour myself a fresh cup of coffee; take a series of deep, cleansing breaths; and pull up a comfortable chair close to the action. Let the games begin!

Not tonight, Joséphine.

NAPOLÉON I (ATTRIBUTED)

B IRDS HAVE THEM. Bees have them. Sex thera-
pists with Ph.D.s have them, to say nothing of
the rest of us overworked, overwhelmed, overextended
mortals. I am talking about dry spells. They happen,
even in the nicest homes. They're among the best-kept
secrets of long-term relationships, and they're nothing to worry about. A nonscientific survey of ten married friends (accompanied by lots of wine and a great
deal of arm-twisting) recently confirmed that at one
time or another, everybody's not doing it. It's just that
nobody's talking about it.

Don't get me wrong. Whatever doesn't take place
between consenting adults in the privacy of their own
home is none of my business. The occasional drought
is simply a fact of married life, like visits from in-laws
and joint tax returns. Try not to take it too personally,
and remember that this, too, shall pass.

But should your little love nest start to resemble Death Valley, you may want to consider the following remedies, from the bedrooms of the Tumbleweed Ten.

- If you can't stand the lack of heat, get out of the bedroom. Changes of scenery can work wonders for tired libidos, and you don't need to leave home to find them. One of our wildest times actually took place on our dog's bed (he was, of course, out at the time). My friend Betsy recommends the play-room floor: "Some women want the wind in their hair during sex. I happen to like LEGOs in my back." If that doesn't do it for you, there's always April in Paris. . . .

- Change your behavior. Become the aggressor, if that's out of character for you, or play the shy, blushing virgin, if it's not. Give your alter ego a name, and refer to her often. Casually mention when she'll be "in town." Vary the script and keep surprising each other. Use appropriate props, if you're able to keep a straight face—or better yet, even if you're not.

- Plant a sexy suggestion at an inopportune mo-ment, then sit back and watch it take root. I never pack my husband off on a sailing trip with the guys without mentioning how horny a sailor can get while at sea. As a result, even his shortest voy-ages seem to end, so to speak, with a bang.

- Bring up previous sexual encounters both of
  you found especially memorable, a sort of replay
  of your own greatest hits. Describe a scintillating
  sex scene from a movie, or read one aloud from a
  book. Conversational intimacy leads to physical
  intimacy, because it stimulates the primary sex
  organ—the brain. Bear that in mind, and you'll be
  walking funny in no time.

Some people suffer in silence
louder than others.

PROVERB

FOR MY HUSBAND, it began innocently enough, with a series of headaches and a sense of fatigue. Then came the blurred vision, and with it, a growing irritability that just wasn't like him at all. That's when he saw me watching him reading the paper, holding it out at arm's length. "I think I need glasses," he told me. There was a terrible look on his face.

My hawk-eyed husband has always prided himself on his ability to see the world clearly, an attribute I've never shared. From the time I was six, I've worn Coke-bottle glasses or contact lenses during all waking hours. Indeed, on the many occasions I've removed my contacts without having my glasses in hand, I've had to summon my husband to fetch them like some two-legged seeing-eye dog.

For the most part, I feel very lucky that my vision is

so easily fixed. But every now and then, usually when we're searching for something—a street, a dropped straight pin, a tick on our mink-coated dog—I can't help but wonder if I am missing something, if life looks different through my husband's brown eyes. Having come to terms with my imperfect vision, I didn't view his needing glasses as any big deal. It wasn't until I noticed him in front of the mirror inspecting the white in his beard that I saw just how blind I had been.

Like that first shot of gray at the temples or the laugh lines that don't go away, those blurry words that appear on the page send a message that suddenly seems all too clear: "You are now leaving your youth and entering middle age. Next stop: heart attacks, hearing aids, canes." We know we're being silly, yet we find we can't help it. It seems the older we get, the faster time travels. The years, like the words, are a blur.

Pretty soon we feel downright decrepit, conscious of each ache and pain. Evidence mounts that we're becoming our parents, with each clue more ominous than the last: Someone asks us our age and we do math before answering. We talk to our friends about 401Ks. We toy with the idea of voting Republican. We realize fried clams give us gas.

"There is something sadder than growing old—remaining a child," wrote Cesare Pavese. For a minute there, we disagree. And yet we refuse to give in to our panic, to treat our middle-aged bodies with kid gloves. Instead, we do for our mates what we hope they will do when it's our turn to squint at the page. We tell them they're a work-in-progress, one that gets better each year. We point out all the ways they have grown since we met. We remind them we love them more every day.

We take them to lunch and from there to the eye doctor, where we help them pick out awesome frames. Our next stop is Herman's for their first pair of Rollerblades, a cheap alternative to a Mazda Miata. Then we turn back into our mothers and insist on protective headgear and plenty of elbow and knee pads. Because there *is* something sadder than growing old, I suspect: spending August in a full-body cast.

> Good communication is as stimulating as black coffee,
> and just as hard to sleep after.

ANNE MORROW LINDBERGH

THEIR NAMES ARE Beth, Jamie, Mary, Erin, Stacey, Teresa, Ann, Lizzie, and Deb, but they prefer to answer to their collective nickname: LNO. Ladies' Night Out. They've been getting together as the need arises for as long as any of them can remember, to drink wine, break bread, and vent their middle-aged spleens about their relationships, their in-laws, their kids, and their jobs.

And while they've had their share of problems, like everyone, the members of LNO are very proud of the fact that they are still married. To Steve, who changed jobs three times in less than two years. To Andrew, who forgot to set the parking brake on the minivan he'd left running at the end of a rather steep driveway. To Joe, who brought home a Newfoundland pup as a total surprise to his wife. To Calvin, who bought his wife a shiny new Electrolux for her fortieth birthday. To John, who . . . well, you get the idea.

And while you might argue it's just a coincidence—the correlation between these women's friendship and the survival rate of their marriages—the participants in LNO beg to differ. For three or four hours every six weeks or so, they get together to laugh and cry about their children's concussions, their men's midlife crises, and each other's acute PMS. Whatever the topic, they always seem to go home feeling happier than they were when they left. Beth credits the wine, and while no one disagrees, in their more thoughtful moments, LNO members talk about empathy, humor, and support. "A situation that's merely annoying when you're by yourself can become a hilarious story provided you have the right audience," Mary says. "Things that used to really get to me no longer do," Stacey adds. "Now, when I have a bad day, I just think of it as raw material for the next episode of Ladies' Night Out."

If it's been a long time since you rubbed elbows with members of your very own species, consider what some time among friends could do for you—and your relationship. Round up your sister, your best friend, your neighbor. Appoint a designated driver or hail a cab, and head someplace fancy, funky, or fun, perhaps the sort of place you haven't been since you left college. Drink some wine, tell some tales, share some secrets. Put a humorous spin on a recent episode from your personal domestic soap opera. Stay up late. Laugh out loud. Eat dessert. Go home with a smile on your lips, a doggie bag in your purse, and the comfort of knowing that you aren't alone.

To live for some future goal is shallow.
It's the sides of the mountain that
sustain life, not the top.

ROBERT M. PIRSIG

I WAS PEERING INTO the depths of the fridge when I noticed it way in the back: the bottle of champagne I'd bought months ago and hidden away, just in case. It was Monday, and I couldn't think of a thing that would justify popping the cork. Neither of us had triumphed at work. It wasn't my birthday or his. Our anniversary was still several long months away. The holidays had all come and gone.

There were all sorts of things we both looked forward to, countless projects we hoped to wrap up. For weeks we'd been talking about them endlessly: "I can't wait until this or that's done." But right now, I realized, happiness was on hold. We were awaiting a reason for joy.

I was still in the fridge with my hand on the bottle

when the phone rang at quarter past six. My husband was calling to ask about dinner and to say he was on his way home. I recited the menu I'd planned to prepare: grilled salmon, fresh corn, and a salad. Then I added that we would be drinking champagne, surprising myself as I said it. "What's the occasion?" he wanted to know. I told him I had no idea. "Well, we'll think of something," he said with a laugh, sounding more upbeat than a moment ago.

By the time he got home, I had hauled out the china and cleared the table of junk mail and books. The grill had been lit and the salad was tossed; the champagne flutes had been rinsed off and dried. And neither of us had come up with a thing that was worth raising our glasses to. I thought long and hard as he opened the bottle and filled both flutes right to the rim. But whatever I thought of was still too far off to merit its own champagne toast.

I looked at him blankly and said I was stumped. Nothing seemed worthy, somehow. Then he smiled and reached out his glass to clink mine. "Here's to the struggle," he said.

The moral, of course, is that any day's a good day to celebrate, so why not pop a cork of your own? There is no better time than right now, after all, to acknowledge the good things in life.

O! that this too too solid flesh would melt.

SHAKESPEARE

MY HUSBAND'S BEEN cheating. I suspected as much. The signs have been there all along. That stain on his collar. His vague answers about his whereabouts during lunch. The circumstantial evidence kept on piling up, and I just kept on letting it slide. I hadn't wanted to believe it, but in my heart of hearts, the truth is, I already knew. Then he got careless, and I could no longer ignore what was happening under my nose.

When I finally confronted him, he didn't try to deny it. "What gave me away?" he inquired. I pointed out the empty potato chip bag wedged under the driver's seat of his car. "How many others have there been? That stain on your shirt..." "Pizza sauce," he whispered. But before I could interrogate him as to his choice of toppings, he noticed the empty Häagen-Dazs ice cream bar wrapper poking jauntily out of the trash. "Well, well. And what have we here?" he asked, his voice filled with righteous indignation. I immediately trotted out the PMS defense, which has served me so well in the past. Not this time, however; I'd apparently overused it this month.

So, OK, we've both cheated and we've both gotten caught. It wasn't the first time, and it won't be the last. Dieting with your spouse is a true test of love, since it brings out the worst in you both. But if your marriage, like mine, is a moveable feast, it's inevitable, a sad fact of life. Having been there and done that countless times in the past, I've adopted this hard-and-fast rule: Get rid of the junk food you cannot resist. Why make it any harder than it is?

Since neither of us coexists well with sweets, not even the ones we don't like, I always tackle the pantry on the eve of D-Day, with a garbage bag and all my resolve. On that evening, we bid farewell to the foods we'll give up with one last meal of pizza or ribs. After that we try hard to be good for a month before taking a break for a day. We try not to turn into diet police, though at various times we both do. But assuming the burden of each other's intake always seems to backfire on us. We also try not to sabotage each other's efforts, even when one of us succeeds and one fails.

Our efforts don't always work out, I'm afraid, even though we keep trying to lose. In fact, we have dieted so many times that our "Farewell to Food Night" has turned into a ritual. Unfortunately, we've spent more time saying farewell than actually being apart. We once spent a whole week eating forbidden foods in anticipation of a diet that never came. Eventually, though, as I walked down Main Street, I had occasion to see my reflection. Who's that person behind me, I thought to myself, then it dawned on me: Uh-oh. It's me.

So we're trying again, and this time we won't quit until every last pound has been lost. At least, that's what we're telling ourselves as we shoulder the burden of doing without. If you, too, are trying to lose a few pounds, try sprinkling extra tenderizer on each other during this difficult and stressful time. Because, as always, you're in it together, and that will be your saving grace. I've known many a woman whose partner can eat his weight—and hers—in the most taboo foods without ever gaining an ounce. There's no way I could live with that guy.

**A sound marriage is not based on complete frankness;
it is based on a sensible reticence.**

MORRIS L. ERNST

M Y HUSBAND CHANGED jobs not that long ago,
and his new colleagues all think he's a peach.
They often make a point of telling him so. They tell me,
too; in fact, I am quite sure they're about to tell me yet
again, over drinks at the grubby bar near his office that
is the unofficial after-hours hangout for his crew. It is
smoky and loud, so loud that this particular colleague
has to shout in my ear to be heard over seventies disco
music that is pulsating out of the jukebox: "YOUR HUS-
BAND IS THE ABSOLUTE GREATEST GUY!"

This is followed in short order by a second opinion,
a veritable dead ringer for the first: "I JUST LOVE YOUR
HUSBAND! HE'S SO WONDERFUL!" A third colleague
nods in agreement as my clearly pleased husband gazes
modestly down at his shoes, the very same shoes that I
trip over nightly as I make my way upstairs to bed. Have

I mentioned that most of his colleagues are women? Really nice, really attractive women, all of whom are considerably younger than I.

It should please me to know he's so well loved at work, and generally speaking, it does. But at the moment I am having a difficult time being reminded how special he is. Because lately Mister Wonderful has been a pain in the butt, grouchy and out of sorts. Not at work, naturally, just at home. I know it's because he's been working too hard and he's totally exhausted as a result. He's also tired of being The New Guy, endlessly amiable, great fun to be with, THE ABSOLUTE GREATEST GUY.

It's a role he plays well, having rehearsed as a child whose father changed jobs the way most guys change oil. (I'm exaggerating, but not all that much.) It was the antithesis of my own childhood, with a father who held one job virtually all his life, living in a house I can still go home to, on a street whose distinguishing potholes and cracks I could diagram with my eyes closed. Whereas my sister-in-law Claudia and I once sat in a car in a subdivision just outside Cleveland listening to our husbands argue over which house they once lived in, the white one, the tan, or the gray. Small wonder he and I view the house we now own through such radically different eyes. Mine fill up with tears at the mere thought of moving, while his scan the real estate ads.

But I digress. Return with me now to the loud, smoky bar where I'm facing a terrible choice. Do I share three or four of his faults with his fans—or shut my mouth and let him have his day? If this seems like a no-brainer, put yourself in my place: your husband is being an absolute saint with everyone who isn't you.

In the end, I do take the high road—not just because it's the right thing to do, but because the woman who rags on her husband in public can only end up looking bad. I can already hear the response from his fans: Too bad his wife's such a bitch! So I suck it up, smile, and agree he's terrific, and ultimately I am glad. Because two weeks from now when I'm back at this bar, one of these women will turn to my husband and bellow, "YOUR WIFE'S AS TERRIFIC AS YOU ARE!"

One of the secrets of a happy life is continuous small treats.

IRIS MURDOCH

W<small>E ARE TAUGHT</small> virtue is its own reward, but given how rewarding its flip side can be, this approach seems a little shortsighted. I'm not saying we shouldn't be good for goodness' sake, only that a little added incentive never hurt anyone, as every good grandparent knows. Childhood, of course, is the "golden age" for rewards, from the cupcakes we get when we finish our green beans to cash inducements for good report cards.

Our need for incentives doesn't end after childhood, but alas, most incentive plans do. Apart from finding lost dogs, fingering dangerous fugitives, or making partner in a profitable law firm, adults have too few opportunities to earn bonuses, treats, or rewards. But it doesn't have to be that way, and for some lucky couples, it's not. They're the ones who've relearned a lesson from childhood, one every five-year-old knows: treats help make life a bit sweeter. And whose life couldn't use a little help?

Take Ethan and Cleo, for example. When they were getting ready to buy their first house, they had to save every last dime. Even with that, they fell short. Based on elaborate calculations, Ethan figured they'd have just enough by the closing, provided they banked every paycheck for the next seven weeks. That meant no new clothes for Cleo, who puts shopping on a par with eating and sleeping.

And yet, somehow, she did it. She avoided the mall, threw away all her catalogs, and hid her copies of *Vogue* in a drawer. And as their bank account grew, she felt more and more proud of having managed to do this hard thing. After the closing, she and Ethan rushed over to tour what was now their new home. Clotheshorse that she is, Cleo made a beeline for the enormous bedroom closet, a key selling point of the house. And there it was—the new suit Ethan had bought her, a reward for having done without for so long.

Like the Lalique perfume bottle Tom bought Jackie when she finally gave up smoking, or the leather jacket Ann bought Sam when he lost twenty pounds, rewards that honor our partners' achievements go a long way toward reinforcing them. But that's only one kind of prize. A special dessert on a weeknight, a sweet note tucked inside a briefcase, or even a warm hug on a cold, rainy day can all boost damp spirits, as can a bowl of hot oatmeal, a back rub, new socks, or a lone Hershey's Kiss in a pocket.

Encouraging messages from my husband on my computer's screen saver have been greeting me in the mornings, making it a little easier to get out of bed and start work. My friend Alex accomplishes much the same thing by sending her husband an e-mail every morning. Janice often sends her boyfriend off to work with a note hidden in one of his pockets.

However you do it, simply or elaborately, take a few minutes today to reward your mate with a small gesture that says "You are special." Remember, no matter how adult we appear on the surface, deep down, beneath the pinstripes or the pantyhose, we're all five-year-olds wishing for cupcakes.

I will not go out with a man who wears more jewelry than me, and I'll never, ever go to bed with a guy who calls me Babe. Other than that, however, I'm real flexible.

LINDA SUNSHINE

WHEN I FIRST met my husband, he sported a gigantic ring on the fourth finger of his right hand, a huge turquoise stone in an ornate silver setting that truly made me want to gag. I sported "big hair," which was fashionable at the time, but which grossed him out totally. He gave up the ring and I gave up the hair. We considered it an even trade.

There remains a vast gray area between us, however, when it comes to our appearances. In it falls all that I love and he hates, and vice versa. Heavy makeup on me. Gaudy plaid shirts on him. The length of my hair and his shorts. Generally speaking, we live and let live, meaning we try not to go to extremes. If, on occasion, I still feel the need to wear eyeliner up to my brows, I put it on with impunity and tell him sweetly, "Tough darts." The same thing holds true for those hideous—oops, make that "colorful"—plaid shirts of his. The rest of the time, we dress up for each other. In other words, we both aim to please.

The feminist in me still finds fault with the way I concede to his preferences. And while I do see her point, it seems counterproductive to dress in a way he abhors. He is, after all, still the person I want to attract and impress and seduce. The fact that we're married shouldn't change that at all. If anything, it should matter more.

So I usually save my "unnatural" look for my nights on the town with the women of Ladies' Night Out, who know a fantastic makeup job when they see one—or who at least know enough to pretend.

**What counts in making a happy marriage is
not so much how compatible you are,
but how you deal with incompatibility.**

GEORGE LEVINGER

OUR FRIENDS John and Patti just sold their
house in New York in order to buy a new boat.
Their plan is to live on the boat year-round. In New
York State. In winter. Oh, my.

I couldn't believe it when my husband first told me,
knowing Patti as well as I do. She's a creature of comfort who loves crackling fires, thick quilts, and a house-
ful of friends. John craves adventure, likes to live on the
edge, and invariably does things his way. I tried to rec-
oncile all this with the thought of my friend keeping
house on a boat. A thirty-seven-foot sailboat, but a boat
nonetheless: close quarters, brisk winds, damp sea air. I
kept drawing a blank, so I picked up the phone and di-
aled their farm in Vermont. "What were you thinking?"
I asked her, aghast. She laughed and said she didn't

know. But it turns out she knew very well what she'd done when she said she'd give John's plan a try.

Most of the time, she'll remain in Vermont, in the farmhouse they bought and rebuilt. John will stay on the boat in New York during the week; on the weekends, they'll meet here or there. "And what happens in January when it's snowing like hell and it's your turn to stay on the boat?" "That's easy," she said, having thought this all through. "On those nights, I'll sleep on your couch."

I saw the new boat a few days after that, and she is a beautiful thing. Sturdy and strong, with teak woodwork, wide berths, and a spacious, utilitarian galley. I could see Patti there, turning out hearty meals and snuggling up with her mate. (I could see wheels turning, too, in my own sailor's head, and I immediately set him straight.) Yet it humbled me, too, to consider the lengths to which Patti was willing to go. A bigger landlubber than I—and that's saying a lot—she is also a much better sport. Which is why she and John fit together so well, even though they are nothing alike. Thinking back over the twenty-odd years I have known them, I can't recall when her good nature failed or when she refused to go along gracefully with one of John's offbeat ideas.

Their happiness has made me wonder if I might be missing something by being too quick to say no. And while I still have no plans to go live on a boat, I could stand to be more flexible. An occasional adventure might be just the thing to keep our marriage from growing too staid. If it's been a long while since you let yourself bend to the wishes or whims of your mate, maybe now is the time to say yes for a change, to show what a good sport you can be.

**Anticipation of pleasure is
a pleasure in itself.**

SYLVIA TOWNSEND WARNER

SOME OF THE most memorable days don't start
out that way. Just yesterday, for example, I was
pawing through my refrigerator in search of something for dinner when I realized all I really cared to
make was a reservation. I booked a table at our favorite neighborhood Italian restaurant, then called
my husband at work to inform him. "Fine. I'll swing
by and pick you up at 7:30," he said. No, I replied, let
me just meet you there. That done, I got on with my
day.

It was a day like a thousand others, except that the
strangest thing started to happen at around six o'clock.
I began to feel oddly elated, almost giddy, if you know
what I mean. I took a shower, put on makeup and
pantyhose, rarities for me these days. But it wasn't until
I dabbed perfume behind my ears that it dawned on me

why I felt this way. I had a date. With my husband! For the first time in a very long time.

Oh, sure, we had been out together—to parties, friends' houses, restaurants. But this was the first time in ages we weren't going together. I was amazed at how different that felt.

For one thing, there was no last-minute impatience, no "Hurry up, c'mon, aren't you ready?" We didn't watch each other dress or critique one another's outfits: "Are you *really* wearing that tie with that shirt?" Best of all, there was nothing to stop me from getting there early, to order some wine and chill out. Opera music played softly in the background when I walked in at seven o'clock. I asked for a table with a view of the door so I could watch as my husband walked through it.

By the time he did, a relaxing half hour later, I wore a grin twice the size of my face. He grinned back like he did in the old days, when we often rendezvoused at coffee shops in the city, stealing the minutes between his shift and mine.

All of that was a very long time ago, but somehow, it seemed less so last night. If you like the idea of making years disappear, try a meet-you-there date with your guy, and see if it doesn't feel different to you. I'd be willing to bet that it will. We drank some more wine with our dinner—salmon for me, pasta for him. Both were good, but to tell you the truth, dinner was beside the point. Because there's nothing more delicious than listening to opera while waiting for someone you love.

O! many a shaft at random sent

Finds mark the archer little meant!

SIR WALTER SCOTT

MOLLY GOT ZINGED by her husband last night. I could tell right away, having been zinged on occasion myself. While zingers aren't always apparent to bystanders, the body language of their intended targets generally gives them away. In this case, Molly crumpled a bit in her chair, and her eyes registered a brief flicker of pain. Gotcha! She was quieter than usual for a while after that. I suspect she was licking her wounds.

Zingers vary from couple to couple, of course, but they're basically verbal assaults: sucker punches aimed deftly below the belt, delivered before witnesses. Any reference to weight gain qualifies as a zinger, as does an acknowledgment of a mate's bad hair day. Generally speaking, they're anything best left unsaid that gets brought up in mixed company. In other words, a breach of the rules.

In Molly's case, the remark concerned the way she is built, and as zingers go, it was a beaut. She was telling us how she'd been dumped by her horse but had managed to land on her butt. Whereupon Andy piped up with an unfortunate joke about the size of our friend's landing site. Thoughtless, unnecessary, and perfectly timed, it was a classic example of the genre. And one, I am sure, Andy lived to regret, the minute he and his wife were alone.

There's a moral here, though, one I'd like to pass on, having studied the form at some length. Zingers do serve a purpose, I've come to believe. The message is basically this: "I am feeling left out, and I'm trying to find a way to participate in this conversation. The only route I can see is directly through you, so heads up, honey. I'm comin' in!" Zingers are a quick way of turning the tables when the attention is focused on you. I'm not condoning them; I'm only saying their primary purpose is not about causing you pain. That just happens to be an unfortunate side effect of the trail that your loved one has blazed. That said, if you happen to sport permanent tread marks in the area south of your belt, it may be time to try out a new strategy aimed at stopping your mate in his tracks.

A friend of mine who has been on the receiving end of more than her share of body blows has come up with an effective catchphrase designed to head zingers off at the pass. When she senses her mate hovering around the perimeter of a conversation he isn't part of, she squeezes his knee and murmurs, "House rules," a reminder to tread carefully. She then tries to escort him into the discussion so he doesn't have to bully his way in. So far, she says, it has worked very well. So why not give her strategy a try? You have nothing to lose but the mortification of being the butt of your butthead's lame jokes.

A lot of friction is caused by half the drivers trying to go fast enough to thrill their girlfriends and the other half trying to go slow enough to placate their wives.

BILL VAUGHAN

I MAY SHARE A house with Dr. Jekyll, but I share two automobiles with Mr. Hyde. Like untold thousands of seemingly mild-mannered men, my husband undergoes a complete transformation the moment he slides behind the wheel. So do his three brothers, gentle souls all—except when they're driving a car. This used to confound me until my sister-in-law reminded me that their late father drove the same way. I, in turn, drive like my father: cautiously, defensively, and within five miles an hour of the speed limit, braking not only for large animals but for birds, turtles, frogs, snakes, and bikes. Which could explain this recent exchange with my beloved:

"Sweetie, your driving really scares me," I said earnestly.

"Well, yours scares me, too," he replied.

"Really?"

"Yeah. I'm scared we'll never get anyplace."

Nor have I managed to get anyplace in my efforts to slow down my mate. Fifteen years of whining and whimpering have had virtually no effect. He continues to tool about town in his aging Toyota like a surgeon en route to a kidney transplant, while I continue to shake in the passenger seat, when I'm not slamming on phantom brakes. As he likes to point out, this gets old very fast, about as fast as a kidney on ice.

So what is a white-knuckle woman to do? She can try asking him nicely to slow the hell down (or stop tailgating, or whatever else drives her nuts), but his response will be temporary at best. "When I say 'You're really scaring me! I feel like we're going to die any minute!' Evan usually slows down," my sister-in-law Claudia reports, "but just for five minutes or so." The following is an abbreviated list of some of the activities my husband's baby brother enjoys as he motors along in excess of the speed limit: chatting with friends and associates on his cell phone, untying and removing his sneakers, and surveying area businesses to check out who's having a sale. "He'll say, 'Oh, look, there's that new restaurant.' And I'll say, 'Gee, I didn't see it because I was watching the road!'"

If you'd rather drive than nag, you could try taking turns, thereby cutting your worry time in half. Since she hates to drive, Claudia brings books along on trips over ten miles or so. There are also crossword puzzles, knitting, and catnaps. And while you may at first find it tough to quit watching the road, I hear it gets easier with time. I hope so, because I am going to try, having realized something I cannot dispute: in all the years that I've known him, my husband has yet to cause an accident or get a ticket. He may just be lucky, but I somehow suspect there's a little more to it than that. Because although he drives faster than I would prefer, he may not be as fast as I think. When he drives, after all, I am not in control, and I do have a hard time with that. We all want to be in the driver's seat, and not just when it comes to our cars. But nobody—at least nobody I'm living with—is apt to let me set the pace all the time.

It takes a certain degree of flexibility to travel through life at somebody else's pace. The sooner we learn how to chill out, I think, the smoother the journey will be. The only alternative is to go it alone, and we've come too far together for that.

Once a woman has forgiven her man,

she must not reheat his sins for breakfast.

MARLENE DIETRICH

WHEN THE NEW Southwestern restaurant earned four stars from the harshest food critic in town, we called our friends Bob and Lisa, fellow "foodies," to see if they wanted to go. It took more than a month to book a table for a Saturday, and by the time the big night rolled around, we were psyched. We walked in to find Lisa already at the bar waiting. Bob would meet us there shortly; he'd had to drop something off at a friend's. No problem. The hostess wouldn't seat us until he'd arrived, so we ordered drinks and sat down to wait. And wait. And wait . . .

After a half hour, Lisa started getting annoyed, but we assured her we weren't in a hurry. Fifteen minutes later, she stomped off in search of a phone. There was no answer at her house or the house Bob was stopping at. By the time he showed up, apologizing profusely for getting held up by his pals after softball practice, the table was no longer ours, and the four of us ended up eating pizza at our usual neighborhood hangout. Though we all made the best of it, once we'd said our good-byes I couldn't help but wonder which couch Bob would be spending the night on: the one in his living room or the one in his den. Either way, it seemed safe to assume he'd be knee-deep in chores for a while, the adult version of being grounded.

Therefore, it came as a shock when Bob called the next morning to see if my husband was free to go sailing. "Sailing! I'm amazed Lisa's letting you out of the house!" I blurted out. A brief silence followed. Then, "I used my jail card," Bob said sheepishly. "Your *what?*" "My get-out-of-jail-free card," he replied. "You know. Like in Monopoly."

It took a few minutes to coax the rest out of him, but Bob's explanation went something like this: Once a year, both he and Lisa are allowed to play their "forgive me" card to be let off the hook for some serious offense—forgetting their anniversary, say, or going out with friends instead of coming straight home as promised. Capital crimes such as adultery, or anything else that does permanent harm to a relationship, are not eligible. The card applies only to the stuff that's more annoying than damaging, the thoughtless, selfish, inconsiderate behavior we're all guilty of displaying every once in a while.

I don't know about you, but I immediately sensed

they were onto something, and so did my better half. We've since adopted a similar policy—as has every couple we've told.

There is a slight catch I should mention. Once the guilty party chooses to relinquish the card, the victim must immediately shut up. No tantrums, no lectures, no nagging, no tears. The debt to the relationship must be marked PAID IN FULL, and the record must then be expunged. Meaning that years from now, when the victim is listing the defendant's previous offenses before a jury made up of her girlfriends, the aforementioned incident must be deemed inadmissible.

Unless, of course, you really can't help yourself and your girlfriends promise they'll never let on.

**He is poor indeed
that can promise nothing.**

THOMAS FULLER

AFTER EIGHT YEARS of living together, our friends John and Susan recently tied the knot in a tiny, no-frills ceremony that mirrored their ambivalence to a T: they did the deed without benefit of flowers, wedding gown, bridesmaids, or rings. The groom trembled perceptibly throughout.

When I ran into them after the fact, they were still looking shell-shocked, still startled by what they had done. John's forty-six, Susan's forty-one, and neither had ever been married. They'd gotten engaged years ago and had decided to leave it at that—not because of any doubts they'd had about each other, but because they have huge doubts about marriage itself. Susan's mother's three marriages had left Susan cynical about the prospect of mating for life. And John considers himself a true nonconformist who prefers to follow a less conventional path.

Nancy Shulins

Their decision to marry dovetailed with a series of other decisions—to quit their jobs, sell their house, and move south. As husband and wife, they thought they might fit in better and find it easier to land jobs and make friends. But neither expected the exchanging of vows to change the way they relate. Aware that couples who live together before marriage have a higher divorce rate than those who don't, John and Susan went to great lengths to keep it all very low-key, and shared the news with just a handful of people.

But while they hadn't wanted it to feel any different, they were startled to find that it did. "There was always a little door off the corner left open," said Susan, "and even though neither of us wanted to use it, we both always knew it was there. Now that we've closed it, we're truly committed, and that changes things for us both." One of the first side effects was a greater willingness to compromise that asserted itself right away. "We used to dig in our heels over little things," Susan said. "I'd want my way and John would want his. Now we're both trying to please one another, so we're more apt to want to give in." She was still trying to determine whether or not this was good, since in their misguided efforts to please one another, they'd done things neither wanted to do. "We'd be finishing a meal at a restaurant neither of us had wanted to go to, and I'd say, 'I thought you wanted to come here,' and he'd say, 'That's funny; I thought you did,'" she said.

There was also this: "I feel like he's more a reflection

of me, like my identity is more tied to his. That was one of the things that kept me from getting married, the idea that my sense of self could get swallowed up." Instead, she said, this melding of identities felt rather pleasant, more like an adding on than a taking away. Throughout their romantic honeymoon in Italy, Susan thought John seemed more protective of her than he had ever been. And she enjoyed introducing him as her husband; that's becoming one of her favorite parts.

Marriage does change you, I have no doubt about that. To expect otherwise is unreal. And the older you are when you marry, I suspect, the more you may find yourselves changed. But as John and Susan are learning together, "different" does not imply "worse." Often it's better. Sometimes you're not sure. But if you panic simply because you think something has changed, you'll have a tough time trying to figure it out. Why not look at marriage as an adventure, a series of discoveries to be made over time. That's what my friends have decided to do, and I can't wait to see what they find.

For now, they're both proud of the step they've taken, publicly stating what they'd known all along: that John and Susan plan to love each other for life. And, as often happens when a door long left open is finally closed, it suddenly feels a lot warmer inside.

> They had quarreled about this single,
> solitary sore point: their life.
>
> ANNIE DILLARD

IT'S THAT TIME again. The forsythia is blooming, the daffodils are up, and the air is filled with a cool April mist. And if you listen closely, you can hear the first strains of the symphony that signals the coming of spring: the sweet melodies of the birds, the insistent chattering of the squirrels, the endless bickering of my true love and me.

Yes, for some reason that makes absolutely no sense whatsoever, now is the winter of our discontent—not January, with its bleak days and long, frigid nights; or February, with its ice storms and accompanying cabin fever; or even March, with its cold winds and deep, sucking mud. No, we prefer April, just as the new leaves unfurl, the azalea buds swell, and the rhubarb bursts forth at the market. The weather turns decent, the carpenter ants parade through our kitchen, and we descend upon each other's throat. Not about anything weighty or crucial or significant in any way. About meaningless stuff. Whose job it is to call up the lawn guy. Whether the fish would be better roasted or grilled. And various things even dumber than that, so dumb that I won't even tell you.

But I will tell you this: marital discord can be seasonal, like hay fever, white sales, and shad roe. I know one couple who fight every Christmas. (They save lots of money this way.) Of course, January is prime time for fights over money, once the holiday bills have arrived. But we're not talking here about fights over issues; we're talking fights over nothing at all.

On second thought, let me amend that. Although no clear-cut themes have emerged, I suspect there is something behind all our squabbles: exhaustion. Depletion. Fatigue. As my husband points out, it's been ages since we went away to relax and have fun. Visits to relatives or tagging along on each other's business trips don't count.

Since neither of us can quite see our way clear to take time off from work at the moment, I'm planning a weekend of fun little things we can do without going away. I haven't decided yet what they will be, but I do know the things we won't do: we won't answer the pager, the phone, or the door; we won't cook or do laundry or chores. In short, we won't do anything resembling work. And neither should you and your mate. The next time an ill wind kicks up outside your door, close it firmly and try chilling out. Spend a whole weekend just goofing off. And if that doesn't stop you from bickering, move right along to plan B, in which you both call in sick Monday morning and pull the covers up over your heads.

Of all the peoples whom I have studied, from city dwellers to cliff dwellers, I always find that at least fifty percent would prefer to have at least one jungle between themselves and their mothers-in-law.

MARGARET MEAD

SHE'S NOT THE person I would have chosen. I would have chosen a person who always says the right thing in the right way at just the right time. Someone who thinks I can do nothing wrong, who takes my side in every fight with my husband. Someone who loves everything about me, who shares my taste, sense of humor, and dress size. In short, I would have chosen somebody perfect. My mother-in-law is not perfect.

I'm not the person she would have chosen. She would have chosen a person who always says the right thing in the right way at just the right time. Someone who thinks she can do nothing wrong, who takes her side in every fight with her son. Someone who loves everything about her, who shares her taste, sense of humor, and dress size. In short, she would have chosen somebody perfect. Her daughter-in-law is not perfect.

And yet, there are times when we clearly forget that we're not the women we would have chosen. When we discover we both loved the same book as kids. When we laugh at the same stupid joke. When I realize there's something I can't wait to tell her, something funny or silly or sad. When she comes bearing gifts not just for me and her son but also for the horse and the dog. There are times when we completely forget the awkward, obligatory nature of the relationship that connects us for life, as two women who both love the same tall, shy man, albeit in far different ways; two women thrown together by legalities and fate, a mother and daughter *in law*.

And if she would have preferred a grandson and granddaughter to a black Lab and a Thoroughbred horse, if she wishes I kept a neater house, fewer secrets, or my rather definite opinions to myself, she never lets on. And if I would have preferred someone a bit more laid-back, with somewhat less energy and drive, as the person with whom I'm compared by my mate, I try not to let that show either.

Because in the lottery of life, I have come up a winner when it comes to my mother-in-law. And given the odds and compared with my friends, I am luckier than I deserve. The chances of finding a wonderful man, let alone a great mother-in-law, are roughly equivalent to finding two four-leaf clovers growing side by side in the same field. Yet I have, and I'm grateful, because, while nobody's perfect, my mother-in-law comes pretty close.

There are homes you run from,

and homes you run to.

LAURA CUNNINGHAM

ANYONE WHO SHARES living space with somebody else knows how annoying cohabitation can
be. All it takes to get your day off to a very bad start is a
small, thoughtless gesture or two: dirty dishes sitting
out on the counter, a carton of milk with just one swal-
low left, an empty toilet paper roll in the bathroom that
you discover a moment too late.

The misdemeanors of marriage add up very fast.
The magazine you left on the table that's gone when
you find time to read it at last. The razor he's asked you
not to use on your legs that turns up in your shower
again. The laundry he promised to put in the dryer that
somehow never quite made the trip. The last English
muffin you'd been saving for breakfast that someone
has eaten for his.

Just the sight of two dirty socks under the table or

an undershirt tossed on the floor can be enough to send your blood pressure soaring or to cause you to mutter and fume. Whoever gets up first can ruin the day for the person who wakes to a mess. Whoever gets home first can ruin the evening of the person who walks in his wake.

Take a minute this morning or evening to check out your house through the eyes of your mate. Look for the little things lying in wait, the stuff he'll see when he walks in the door. Throw it all in a shopping bag if you don't have time to put everything in its proper place. Send a welcoming message to your nearest and dearest, one that tells him you're glad he came home.

**A person who has no secrets is a liar.
We always fold ourselves away from others
just enough to preserve a secret or two,
something that we cannot share without
destroying our inner landscape.**

ANNE ROIPHE

W E HAVE NO secrets; we tell each other everything." So begins an old Carly Simon song, one
I used to play all the time. I have no idea who she is
singing about, but I do know this: it isn't us.

Just about everybody I know keeps some secret, particularly from his or her mate. I'm not talking about
anything earth-shattering here, nothing life threaten-
ing, scandalous, or bad. I'm referring to small guilty
pleasures, the sort we all allow ourselves now and then.
The hours we spend playing solitaire on our laptops
while pretending we're paying the bills. The little food
vices best savored in secret—our "dietary indiscretions,"
so to speak. The Marlboro we bum from a friend at the

bar, the "adult" magazines he hides in his drawer. The stuff that, revealed, would play havoc with our perceptions of our nobler selves.

We leave clues now and then to our closet indulgences, like the stray candy wrapper that litters the car. The compassionate spouse knows enough to ignore them, to tacitly allow an indulgence or two. It is one of the unwritten rules of marriage that we all would do well to observe, because no one likes being scrutinized by somebody else, least of all someone we love. And because the person whose small, harmless secrets are denied may instead choose to hide something big.

I once knew a woman who spied on her mate in various unsavory ways. She went through his dresser and searched all his pockets; she scrutinized credit card slips. She checked out his phone bills and cross-examined his buddies. She tracked his movements during his business trips.

I asked her once what she was looking for, and she replied, "Anything I can find." She found all sorts of little, innocuous things and confronted him with every last one. After three years of this, she found her smoking gun: a receipt for a necklace he'd purchased that she'd never gotten. She confronted him with the evidence, and he broke down and confessed to having recently had a brief fling. She cried and sulked, he ranted and raved, and they ended up in marriage counseling. Then he got a new job and they moved out of state. Eventually, we lost touch.

I felt bad for her when it happened, yet it was obvious she'd egged him on. She looked so hard for trouble that she eventually found some, and I think there's a lesson in that. Had she let him keep a few harmless things to himself, it's possible he wouldn't have strayed.

I think of her still, every now and again, when I find evidence of some small vice of my mate's. I then bite my tongue and put it back where I found it, someplace hidden, where it's hurting no one.

> Sometimes I wonder if men and women
> really suit each other.
> Perhaps they should live next door and
> just visit now and then.
>
> KATHARINE HEPBURN

DINNER MAY BE a while. I just saw my husband head into the bathroom with volumes *J* through *P* of the *Encyclopaedia Britannica*.

OK, I'm exaggerating; it was only a sailing magazine, a computer software manual, and last Sunday's *New York Times Magazine*. But as long as we're on the subject, what *is* it with men and their bathrooms? What's taking them so long, anyway?

I took the question to a panel of experts and discovered the following: Bathrooms are to men as day spas are to women—holy places far removed from ringing phones, traffic jams, and other hassles of everyday life. They're also reference libraries, reading rooms, chapels, and studies; hair salons, shopping malls, cafés, and retreats. For every minute a woman spends in her bathroom, the average man spends about thirty—forty if the new Home Depot circular has just arrived.

Men spend more quality time with their plumbing than they do with their significant others, with the possible exception of their personal home computers. In fact, my sister is convinced that if someone were to invent a toilet seat that fit under a PC, she'd never see her man again. Unfortunately, he wasn't available to comment on this, having sequestered himself in his bathroom along with three *Time* magazines, two old copies of *Movieline*, and the January issue of *MacWorld.*.

Last I knew, he was still in there. But if he comes out for Christmas, I'll get back to you.

Chains do not hold a marriage together.

It is threads, hundreds of tiny threads,

which sew people together through the years.

SIMONE SIGNORET

WE ALL HAVE days now and then when we find ourselves looking skyward, wondering what we could possibly have done to so anger the gods, and what we might do to appease them. I seem to be having just such a day today, and I've got the skinned knee, strewn groceries, and spilled coffee to prove it. But I also have just the thing to rid myself of the curse that has plagued me throughout my morning: I shall call up my husband and have him say "Rabbit, rabbit," and then I'll repeat it back to him. If only we'd remembered to say it fourteen days ago, I would never have had all these mishaps.

My "rabbit, rabbit" ritual is my own little hedge against the forces of darkness that trip women and tear their grocery bags (that is, klutziness and an unwillingness to double-bag). My words probably won't reach the gods' ears, but they will reach my husband's, thereby eliciting the spousal empathy that will help turn my outlook around. Because nothing seems quite as bad when there's someone to share it, someone to listen and care. Not just the big things but the daily minutiae, the small disasters of everyday life: the snarled traffic, burned toast, and sudden downpours. The umbrellas that blow inside out.

Who can say how these rituals get started—or even more puzzling, how they become part of our lives? I only know that when we both say "Rabbit, rabbit" on the first of each month, before either of us says another word, we breathe a sigh of relief, having gotten the month off to a good start. Along similar lines, neither of us would feel comfortable heading off on a business trip without hearing the other say "Everything carefully," a general admonition that covers the traveler's safety in the air and on land and sea. Nor would we undertake any difficult challenge without grinding our fists together and making a *shhhh* noise, like the sound of running water—our oddball way of saying "good luck."

Silly superstitions? Absolutely. And yet our rituals do have certain magical powers. Not to protect us, of course, nor to ensure our success. No, their magic lies elsewhere, in their ability to make us feel better by reminding us that we have each other. To commiserate on our bad days. To feel our absence when we go away. To encourage us from the sidelines. To love us more—come what may—every day, coffee stains, torn bags, and all.

If only we'd quit trying to be happy,
we could have a pretty good time.

EDITH WHARTON

THERE'S A LOVELY Spanish restaurant right near our house that serves the world's greatest seafood paella. Years ago, when we first moved here, it was housed in a strip mall and we used to go there on the spur of the moment, whenever we needed a boost. It was the sort of place that you try to keep secret: great food, moderate prices, reservations not required. Well, the secret got out and the restaurant moved to a considerably more upscale address. The critics raved, the prices soared, and now folks wait weeks to get in.

Four times we ate at the new place, and four times we wound up having fights. We now refuse to go anywhere near it. These days, we go to a little Italian place back at the strip mall where there's never a wait to get in. The service is glacial, but we always have fun, unlike the swell, pricey place across town.

I'd forgotten all about our bad restaurant karma until recently, when a group of us decided to go out. Claire and I were assigned to come up with a place, and I suggested the Old Black Goose Grille. "No, Gerry and I always fight there," Claire said. I mentioned the Cuban place next. Claire got back to me two hours later. "No dice," she reported. "Sara and Ted had a big fight there Friday, and Sara said never again."

I always thought it was just us, but it turns out to be everyone—everyone who's ever heaped tons of pressure on themselves to go have the time of their lives. Not only at dinner, but on birthdays and anniversaries, vacations and romantic getaways. I'll never forget the moment midway through our honeymoon when my husband of four and a half days turned to me and said, "Let's go home." Not exactly the three little words a new bride longs to hear, but I pretty much felt the same way. We stuck it out despite horrible head colds and were ultimately glad we did, but neither of us remembers that trip very fondly. We've since taken lots of vacations that follow this general rule of thumb: the lower our expectations, the better the time, which also explains why we never fight at the diner. We save up our hostility for La Côte Basque or Chez Panisse, nice low-key places like that. As the saying goes, you can dress us up, but you can't take us out.

Conversely, we've had many good times back at home in our sweat pants, eating Chinese takeout or washing the dog. Freed from the burden of unrealistic expectations, it's amazing how much fun you can have. With that in mind, I've devised a new strategy for those high-pressure nights on the town, one you may try with your partner. Simply have sex *before* you have dinner. That way, everything else will be gravy.

**It takes a loose rein to
keep a marriage tight.**

JOHN STEVENSON

Y HUSBAND WENT sailing Saturday afternoon
with a woman whom I've never met. They left at
lunchtime and got back after eight; I had opted to stay
home and work. It was a great day to sail, he reported
that night, and they both had a wonderful time. They
dropped anchor off Long Island and swam in the
Sound, then had lunch on the boat and sailed home.
Trusting my husband as much as I do, it never dawned
on me to be concerned. In fact, I didn't give it a thought
till my grandmother called on the phone for a chat
Sunday night. "Did the two of you take out the boat
over the weekend?" she wanted to know. "He did," I
replied. "I stayed home." Then she happened to ask
who had gone out with him, and I told her. Then she
said, *"Aha!"*

"Don't be silly," I said, but her tone lingered on in

my mind for the rest of the night. Should I have been bothered by the thought of my husband's sailing off with some babe who's not me? I don't think so, and yet there's a part of me that feels uncomfortable with the idea. Not a big part, just enough to keep this on my mind four days after the fact.

I don't much like the feeling, but I'm not about to tell him I'd rather he not do it again. Because I know what he'd say: "Don't you trust me?" "Yes, of course," I'd reply. "It's not that." But the truth is, it's all about trusting him; therefore, I'm choosing to keep my mouth shut. I've ridden enough horses to know what occurs when you try to choke up on the reins. They pull and they chafe and they paw at the ground, and you lose your connection with them.

And while this may strike you as an oddball comparison, I think most creatures respond the same way. None of us likes the feeling of being controlled; it only encourages us to rebel. Since my husband has never given me cause for concern, my insecurity has its roots in my past, when I dated less decent, less trustworthy types. It's not fair to restrict him for reasons that have nothing to do with the two of us now. The time to look over my shoulder has long since come and gone. That was then, as they say. This is now.

But I will take my shakiness as a sign that I need to spend quality time with my mate. The next time he offers to take me out sailing, I won't be so quick to say no. If you, too, find yourself feeling a bit insecure for reasons that are rooted in the past, try not to let them interfere with the present. Instead, plan something fun to share now. The more good times we have with our partners, the stronger our connection with them. With men, as with horses, it just doesn't work to rely on a tightly held rein. That only gives the illusion of safety; real security comes from within.

**There are times when sympathy is
as necessary as the air we breathe.**

ROSE PASTOR STOKES

M Y FRIEND PAT often speaks of a curious game
that her family played over dinner. Someone
would bring up a recent illness or injury, describing it
in loving detail. "Hell, that's nothing," someone else
would reply. The challenger would proceed to detail *her*
symptoms with an eye toward outdoing the first. Any
number of people could participate, Pat explained, but
her father invariably won. He'd wait until everyone else
had a turn, then he'd jump in and play the trump card.
"You don't know what pain is," he'd begin.

It wasn't until she had left home for good that Pat realized how warped all this was. It took her years to undo
the distortion the game had brought to her worldview.
She once told me the greatest lesson she'd learned as an
adult was that life needn't be a suffering contest.

Most of us know this, and yet we still play our own

versions of Pat's childhood game. We vie with our mates to see who is more needy, more resentful, or more out of sorts. Who's more overworked? More depleted? Who had the yuckier day?

Once my husband and I start comparing misfortunes, we tend not to know where to stop. We race each other right down the stairs of our psyches until we both hit the depths of despair. (We play the Headache and Exhaustion Edition of the suffering game; my sister and her husband prefer Cold and Flu.)

The problem with "You Don't Know What Pain Is," is that nobody knows where to stop. That's because dueling hardships are hard-pressed to make us feel better. Especially when all most of us *really* want is a little sympathy (and perhaps a stiff drink).

The next time your partner comes home feeling unhappy, resist the temptation to see his bad day and raise him a backache. Forfeit your turn and console him instead. Your bad day will come by and by.

If you're going to be able to
look back on something and laugh about it,
you may as well laugh about it now.

MARIE OSMOND

W E'RE HAVING A heat wave. A tropical heat
wave. For the past three days, the temperature
has soared to one hundred degrees and beyond, with
the sort of humidity that drives meteorologists into a
frenzy of explanations about heat indices and prompts
endless articles in the newspaper urging readers to
check on the elderly. The air is both visible and chewy,
and on the rare occasions when I am forced to open the
door of the bedroom, the only air-conditioned room in
the house, my dog fixes me with a withering look. If he
could speak, he'd say: "Must you?"

Unfortunately, I must. Despite the heat, there are
still dirty clothes to be washed, groceries to be bought,
and work to be done, in a house that with each passing
day feels a bit more surreal and grotesque. The heat

wave coincided with a holiday weekend, and the fact that all three of us, canine included, survived in this withering hothouse is a testament to the power of humor. Without it, any number of moments could easily have turned out to be our last: when I opened the refrigerator and a bowl containing approximately five hundred cherries leaped out in a suicide attempt, when my husband walked in the door soaked with sweat from a fruitless search for a second air conditioner, when the power went off—and stayed off—for five hours while we gently poached in our own sweat.

When things get this bad, you have only two choices. You can laugh your head off or you can cry. We decided to laugh, and it helped us stay sane—not that it couldn't have gone the other way. In borderline situations, the tone gets set early on, usually with the very first mishap. When the pizza falls topping side down on the floor, then gets stepped on by husband and dog. When the sewer backs up in your basement just as your weekend house guests arrive. When you take the dog out for a walk late at night and you're both sprayed point-blank by a skunk. All this and much more has happened to us, and we are still husband and wife. Because in the instant in which these things happened, when we hovered on the brink of despair, one of us managed to say something funny. The other one managed to laugh.

**One advantage to marriage, it seems to me,
is that when you fall out of love with him,
or he falls out of love with you, it keeps you
together until you maybe fall in love again.**

JUDITH VIORST

I N EVERY RELATIONSHIP there comes a time when
we wonder what we ever saw in each other. When the
magical quality of our courtship seems but a vague, distant memory. When the mannerisms we usually view as
so charming are suddenly causing us to grind our teeth.

Today is just such a day for my friend Betsy, who arrived on my doorstep bright and early to vent. "I *hate*
my husband," she told me, with a vehemence that startled us both. She doesn't, of course, and she knows it.
But that was the last thing she wanted to hear. For the
third year in a row, Steve had missed their daughter's
piano recital when a business trip scheduled for two
days had stretched into three. And for the third year in
a row, Betsy had borne the brunt of it. By the time Steve

got home, all was forgiven, by his daughter but not by his wife. And while Betsy knew, deep inside, that it wasn't his fault, she was having a terrible time letting go of her anger.

Why didn't our mamas tell us there'd be days like this, when we can't stand the sight of our darlings? When grotesque crimes of passion actually start to make sense. When we're scared to death by our own anger, because it blocks out our feelings of love.

We don't feel comfortable thinking about such things, let alone saying them to our girlfriends out loud, which is why our mothers never told us the truth: that there *are* days like this, and they're just part of life. They are rare and infrequent, but to pretend they don't happen makes us feel more alone when they do.

And they can be revelations, these bad days, for they can lead to a deeper definition of love, provided we remain calm and don't give in to panic. That's easier said than done, as my friend Jane discovered when a nasty fight with her partner, Randy, mutated love into hate. Bags packed, she was halfway to the door when he blocked it. He was as bewildered as she was enraged. "I thought my anger meant it was all over for us," says Jane, who met Randy three years after her first marriage ended in divorce. "I used to think that in order to love someone, you had to *always* feel love for that person, every minute of every day."

She now knows that a couple can survive a bad day, week, or even year with their commitment and love still intact. And knowing that has made her more secure in her marriage. "The last time Randy and I came through a rough stretch, we looked at each other, laughed somewhat shakily, and said Thank God that's over. Then we brushed ourselves off and went on."

A willingness to brush off the bad times is essential for any relationship, especially one that's to last us a lifetime. Those of us who are unable to do so wind up carrying all that anger around until its cumulative weight drags us down. Loving more every day means learning to let go of that baggage, to brush ourselves off and go on. Perhaps we need to create our own "making up" rituals to help us do that, little ceremonies or rites that reinforce who we are when we're at our best as a couple: a kiss on the head, just to say "I still love you." Candlelit bubble baths, followed by lovemaking. Moonlit walks under the stars. Anything that reminds us of each other's value, even on our most difficult days.

The truth is, lasting love is a complex, paradoxical business. Like nature, it's constantly changing. It waxes and wanes, ebbs and flows, much like the moon and the tides. Love may even vanish from sight on occasion, cloaked in darkness or hidden by clouds. But it's there, even when we can't see it. Just like the moon, it's still there.

This is the urgency: Live!

And have your blooming in the noise of the whirlwind.

GWENDOLYN BROOKS

MARJORIE'S HUSBAND OF thirty-three years passed away two months ago. His name was Martin, and he choked to death on a slice of whole wheat toast at a day care center not far from their house. Since Alzheimer's disease had stolen the essence of him long before his body died, Marjorie never realized she'd find this so hard to live through. But there is more to a husband than intellect, after all. There is also the smell of his skin and the feel of his arms, the familiar, comforting landscape of his body. She had thought it might be a relief when he died. Instead, she finds herself in a deeper abyss.

Five years had passed since her husband got sick, though the first signs were subtle and strange. He stopped tuning in to the *McNeil-Lehrer Report* and started watching *Hard Copy* instead. And he forgot certain things, as does everyone else. As a nurse, Marjorie took note of these behavioral changes, but none of them warranted a 911 call. Who thinks of Alzheimer's in someone so young? For the longest time, nobody did. But then he got fired for mistakes on the job, and his illness could not be denied. Marjorie hadn't known he'd been in trouble at work, since Martin hadn't mentioned a word.

That was the day they'd begun all the tests, which went on for a matter of years. By the time Martin's Alzheimer's disease was confirmed, he was already severely impaired. But with Marjorie's help, he could still live at home, surrounded by trappings of his former life. If you didn't know he was sick, he could fool you, and so, for the longest time, I didn't know. They were just another couple out walking their dog at the park where I often walk Jake. If something about Martin made you stop and look twice, it was only his silver beard and his fine, handsome face, his impeccable clothes and his runner's physique.

He ran every morning, like always, until a neighbor reported to Marjorie that he'd urinated in her front yard. After that Marjorie went with him, and she explained his illness to some of the people on his route. Every evening on her home computer, she made him a new greeting card. They were waiting for him when he woke up each day; he could still read the messages inside.

As his illness progressed, Martin's children closed

ranks, helping Marjorie whenever they could. But it soon reached the point where she needed a break, and day care seemed like a godsend to her. For a few hours a day, she could turn her attention to something besides her sick mate, who was rapidly becoming more of a child than a man, even though physically he was unchanged. Her depression grew deeper as her husband's world shrank. But even so, there were occasional moments that transcended the horror for her.

Like the bus driver who brought him to day care every morning, on a bus filled with barely functional adults. Since Martin hadn't wanted to get on the bus, Marjorie appealed to her husband's work ethic, pretending he was going off to his job, and the bus driver played along. He acted the part of a limousine driver and treated Martin like the man he once was, a busy executive about to jump on a plane for a crucial meeting with business associates. There were signs that Martin may have been blissfully unaware of the illness devouring his brain, like the day Marjorie mentioned needing to look for a job and he asked her, "For you or for me?"

One night when he'd pestered her endlessly for the dinner she was struggling to fix, she seated him at the table with paper and pen and told him to write her a note. "I make you a card every day," she had said. "Now it's your turn to make one for me." She still cries when she thinks of the sentence he wrote, in a child's scrawl she could barely make out: "I love you, and I couldn't live without you." One final message from the person she married had managed somehow to get through.

She still has the note, and the memories of him as he was before he'd gotten sick. She is grateful for their good years, their children, their love. Like so many couples who marry quite young, their paths had diverged for a time. He'd focused on work, and she'd focused on kids, but somehow they'd found their way back. And they'd found they still loved who they'd grown up to be, even though they had both changed a lot. "We didn't wait till we retired to spend quality time. We went places, we made time to live life. Given the way everything has turned out, that's really the biggest blessing of all." It's easy to postpone enjoyment in life, but time sometimes runs out on us. Don't wait till it's too late to realize your dreams. No one knows what the future will bring.

The last time I saw them before Martin died, Marjorie shared what his doctors had said: that with his runner's heart, he was still in great shape, that he'd probably live on forever. She takes comfort in knowing a part of him will—forever vibrant and safe in her heart.

The only real security is not insurance or money or a job, not a house and furniture paid for, or a retirement fund, and never is it another person. It is the skill and humor and courage within, the ability to build your own fires and find your own peace.

AUDREY SUTHERLAND

I TOOK JAKE TO the park this morning to frolic alongside his species, and he did something he seldom does: he let a golden retriever climb on top of him, with nary a snarl or complaint. I chalked it up to the fact that he feels insecure, the result of an unfortunate incident that took place at this same park last week. A dalmatian attacked him as he lay in the shade, biting his ear till it bled. I am sure the bite hurt, but what hurt even more was the blow to my dog's self-esteem. His confidence suffered, and as a result, he no longer fancies himself the top dog.

I can relate to this somehow, since I, too, am feeling a bit insecure these days. In the slow dance of marriage,

Every Day I Love You More

I am lagging behind, letting my mate take the lead. It goes back and forth on the dance floor of life, subtly shifting each day. Sometimes I spin him around and around, twirling and dipping with ease. Other times I am the one following, keeping time to the rhythm he sets. Who leads and who follows on each given day can depend on a great many things, including our relative vulnerability and state of mind; even illness and fatigue play a role. Often, whoever is doing the best job at work is the dominant partner at home. That's what is happening now, I believe. He just got a raise, whereas I'm struggling mightily to write a book due in a month. It is not coming easily, nor is there anyone stroking my ego right now. It's just me and my animals day after day. That, and the dreaded blank page.

Insecurity waxes and wanes in a marriage, just as it does in a life. But in both life and marriage, we must look to ourselves for the confidence that we all seek, because external sources are unreliable at best, and because, ultimately, we're all we have. And when we cease to be there for ourselves, you can bet we won't be there for anyone else. So it's up to me now to take myself by the hand, to build my own fires and find my own peace. I may make a list, corny as it sounds, of the qualities in myself I like best. Or review past achievements by replaying my mental CD of my own greatest hits. I may even take myself shopping for something wonderful to pamper myself: body lotions, new makeup, a facial. Whatever it takes to feel better about me is what I'm planning to do with my day. And once I've relocated my strong, inner self, I'll come home to share it with my husband.

Why not take a few minutes today for yourself to write down your own attributes? It's a present that you alone can give yourself, a lasting, invaluable gift. Keep it where you can refer to it often, when you're insecure or just feeling down. Strength and humor and courage are inner resources that help us through every tough day. And while nobody else hands them over to us, neither can anyone take them away.

**One must not be mean with affections;
what is spent of the funds is renewed in the spending
itself. Left untouched for too long, they diminish
imperceptibly or the lock gets rusty; they are there,
all right, but one cannot make use of them.**

SIGMUND FREUD

WE USED TO hold hands as we walked down the street, but we rarely do that anymore. There was a time when we greeted each other with a kiss, but we now sometimes just say hello. And while I remember the days when I demanded a hug before letting him walk out the door, I find myself hollering "See ya tonight!" when he's upstairs and I'm heading out.

What happens when we have been married awhile? What becomes of those kisses and hugs? Through some insidious process, they tend to diminish even as the years multiply. Long, soulful kisses become pecks on the cheek; heartfelt hugs turn to pats on the arm. Then even the pecks and the pats disappear, until not touching becomes the norm. I'm not talking about having sex when I say this; I am talking about physical affection.

I can't speak for you, but I've caught a glimpse of the future, and frankly, it doesn't look good. On my way to the dog park last evening, I saw an elderly couple out on the town. They were dressed up, at least for a Sunday, and appeared to be en route to dinner or a show. What caught my eye, though, as they walked along the sidewalk, was the fact that they were holding hands. There's no statute of limitations on signs of affection; it's just a matter of remembering to reach out.

Starting tonight, I will once again reach for his hand when we walk down the street. When we sit across from each other at dinner, I'll look in his eyes instead of my magazine. When he comes home from work, I will give him a hug, regardless of how busy I am. And I'll keep doing these things until they become automatic, the way it was when our romance was new. Withholding affection is a habit. And so is showering it on the person we love.

**A grown-up is a child
with layers on.**

WOODY HARRELSON

LIKE FAVORITE UNCLES, eccentric millionaires, and almost all master pastry chefs, your relationship has an inner child, a playful, mischievous spirit that flatly refuses to grow up. It's up to you and your partner to recognize it, nurture it, and take it places, like Disneyland, where you stand the best chance of coaxing it out. In return, it'll keep showing up when you need it, reminding the two of you never to stop being playmates even as you're busy being partners, parents, and friends.

We all have periods in our lives when life seems a little too real. When too many of our waking hours seem to be spent slogging from task to task and chore to chore. When our responsibilities to our families, our homes, and our jobs siphon off every ounce of our energy, leaving us overwhelmed and depleted and desperately in need of some fun. That's when we look to our inner child to rescue us from the burdens of adult existence, if only for an hour or two. Like the snowy afternoon we transformed a steep driveway into a neighborhood luge run. Or the summer night we took turns pushing each other in a swing fashioned from a discarded tire. Or the Halloween we took our black Lab trick-or-treating disguised as a chubby dalmatian.

Unfortunately, the typical inner child is petrified of loud voices, Mylanta, and severe PMS, and therefore goes into hiding in times of stress. Should this happen to yours, you may need to acquire a dog, whip up some cupcakes, or initiate a pillow fight, since no inner child can resist any of these. Our relationship's inner child is a sucker for snowball fights, Mallomars, and New Year's Eve noisemakers, not to mention Saturday morning cartoons, make-your-own sundae bars, and anything whatsoever having to do with Christmas. It likes water, too; we've never known it to miss out on a trip to the beach or a long, soggy walk in the rain. And on those rare summer days when we wash our cars in our driveway, it can be counted on to steal the hose and get us both soaked.

As with real children, our relationship's inner child is often irresponsible. It's the first to suggest calling in sick, staying up late, and shoving a mess in the closet. On the other hand, it's great at entertaining our nieces and nephews, making up silly games to play with the dog, and enhancing our parties by inviting too many people, cranking up the music, and insisting on something gooey and chocolatey for dessert. In short, our relationship's inner child has tons of redeeming value. If it were to leave, I would miss it and so would my husband, because without it, we'd have to be grown-ups all the time, and I doubt any marriage could take that.

This week, why not take a short break from the hassles of life as a grown-up? Make a play date with your partner. Head for the hills with a Flexible Flyer. Build a snow fort and take on some kids. See a Disney movie, visit a planetarium or the zoo, or head for a kid-friendly restaurant. Refuse to even *look* at a vegetable. For that matter, eat dessert first.

**One of the oldest human needs is
having someone to wonder where you are
when you don't come home at night.**

MARGARET MEAD

NORMALLY I WALK the dog during the day and my husband takes him out at night, but since I had a book to drop off at my neighbor's, I offered to take him last night. It was a beautiful evening, not too hot for a change, and dozens of people were out. We stopped to play with a boxer dog on the next street, and the two Bernese mountain dogs after that. We were gone quite awhile, though I didn't realize how long till my husband drove up in his car. "Where have you been?" he demanded. The look on his face warmed my heart.

I apologized to him for worrying him, but to be honest, it made me feel good. Having someone come after you when you're delayed sends a message of love and concern. That he'd walked away from his favorite TV show to look for me made me appreciate it even more. I'd never do it on purpose, but on those rare occasions when I can't call him to say I'll be late, I'm reminded of just how important it is to have someone to worry and wait.

There was a time in my life when I lived by myself and could come and go just as I pleased. The freedom was fun and I took advantage of the fact that nobody kept tabs on me. If I felt like going out with some friends after work, there was no one I needed to call. Nor was there anyone pacing the floor or watching the clock or the door. It was great while it lasted, but now that it's over, I find I don't miss it at all. A phone call to say I'll be late getting home seems an awfully small price to pay for having somebody waiting who cares.

Connections are truly what life's all about, even if they cramp our style at times. When the ties seem to bind me instead of embrace, I just picture that look on his face, that where-have-you-been-I-was-worried expression, the one that makes me feel cherished, not chafed.

In this era of cell phones, it's easy to take a few minutes to check in at home. If you haven't been doing this, try it and see if it doesn't add to your quality of life. It could also mean the difference between getting stuck all alone and having somebody come rescue you.

What we lack is not so much leisure to do
as time to reflect and time to feel.
What we seldom "take" is time to experience the things
that have happened, the things that are happening,
the things that are still ahead of us.

MARGARET MEAD AND RHODA METRAUX

A GIRLFRIEND OF MINE is taking her children to
Martha's Vineyard for three weeks in July. The
first week, she's hosting her sister, with nieces and
nephews in tow. The second week belongs to her in-
laws; her husband is joining them then. Her parents are
planning to spend the third week of vacation with her
and her kids. She plans to let everyone fend for themselves; she vows not to act as their maid. Knowing her as
I do, I find this tough to believe. The words *pipe dream*
keep coming to mind.

Vacations are tricky, especially for those who have
trouble leaving loved ones behind. But the idea of get-

ting away means just that: putting distance between you and them. "Them" as in children and in-laws and pets. "Them" as in siblings and friends. "Them," now and then, may include your own spouse, although that depends on where you are going.

For couples who don't get much time to themselves, it's crucial to pack up and go. At least once a year, although twice is ideal. You deserve it, and so does your mate. Visiting relatives isn't getting away, even if your aunt lives in Tahiti or France. Furthermore, staying with friends doesn't count. The idea is to be by yourselves. You can meet friends for dinner, or breakfast, or lunch, but no guest rooms or foldaway couches. If that means you can afford only a few days, you're still better off in a hotel.

You may bring one small bag, plus a camera and film. Let the hotel do laundry for you. Pack bathing suits, underwear, shorts, a black dress. Leave everything else behind. Makeup is optional. Pantyhose, too. Don't even think about bringing your laptop. Go someplace warm, with great tropical drinks. Hang out on the beach, then go dancing. Take a camping trip or a road trip with no destination. Forget you have children for three or four days. Call if you must, but no cell phones.

Lose all your baggage (figuratively speaking, that is). Let the whole world consist of just you. Get away from the noises that drown out the sound of a universe made up of two.

The difference between courtship and
marriage is the difference between the pictures
in a seed catalogue and what comes up.

JAMES WHARTON

M Y FRIEND MARTHA and I had a game we would
play as young girls while we walked home together from school. We'd gaze into the future and
imagine ourselves all grown up, living life side by side.
Our children would play together, as would our dogs,
while we drank coffee and churned out bestsellers. Our
rich, handsome husbands would be off at work, writing
symphonies and transplanting hearts, but they'd always stop to buy roses on their way home for dinner
(coq au vin, with chocolate mousse for dessert).

The details changed with the times—at some point
the composer morphed into a rock star—but I kept on
playing right into adulthood, even though Martha had
moved far away. By the time I walked down the aisle
(not an aisle at all, but the front porch of an old coun-

try inn), I'd spent more than two decades inventing the details of my happily married life.

Every now and then, more than fifteen years later, I still catch myself measuring the distance between then and now. I look at my marriage, my husband, my life, and I think: This is not what I pictured. Where are the children? The roses? The mousse? Then my gaze shifts to what's there instead.

I can't remember the last time my husband sent flowers, but just this week he came home with a gift. Jake and I had gone out front to greet him, and I could tell it was coming by the look on his face. He reached into his black bag and pulled it out with a flourish: a big piece of clear bubble wrap. Jake ran over to sniff it and my husband popped one of the bubbles; Jake lunged forward and barked wildly. This went on a few more times, until Jake sank his teeth into the plastic, popping bubble after bubble as he bit. By this time he'd gotten the hang of the game and was zooming around at top speed with the bubble wrap in his mouth and the two of us, in hysterics, at his heels. You probably had to be there, but trust me on this: it was the most fun I'd had in a week.

Small surprises and unexpected pleasures are the Miracle-Gro of a marriage, helping it blossom and thrive. Like your houseplants, your marriage still needs to be fed in order to stay in top form. When I mentioned this to my husband, he said he understood just what I meant. Then he reminded me of one day last summer when I'd placed a ripe peach in his hand. "Here," I said. "Smell something wonderful that you haven't smelled for a whole year."

"It was big and fat and juicy," he recalled. "I smelled the stem end and it smelled like heaven on a summer day. The peach itself affected me strongly, but I also felt a wave of love and appreciation for you for having pointed it out to me." And when he told me the story, I felt a wave of love too, that he'd remembered it so well for so long.

So there you have it, one couple's secrets for staying together: bubble wrap and a ripe peach. After all, it's the little things as much as the big things that hold people together over the years. And no fictional marriage can ever compete with the real one that takes root and grows.

No, this isn't the marriage I pictured. But this is the marriage I have. Challenging, frustrating, comforting, loving, evolving with every new day. As surprising as a bouquet of bubble wrap; as rich as a ripe summer peach.

Grow old along with me!
The best is yet to be.

ROBERT BROWNING

FIFTY YEARS AGO this month, Sara Lee introduced frozen cheesecake, the National Basketball Association was formed, *Death of a Salesman* opened on Broadway, and a bushy-haired frat man from the University of New Hampshire took a shy, skinny Rhode Island girl to be his lawfully wedded wife at one of the swankiest affairs Wrentham, Massachusetts, had ever seen, right down to the cherries jubilee.

A quart of milk cost a dime when my parents got married; their first house went for twenty-two grand. Bill Clinton wore diapers; my mom wore a dress I'm unable to pull up past my knees. The conventions of marriage were every bit as constricting as Mom's ivory satin wedding gown. Men held the jobs, women held babies, and no one had ever heard of the Pill.

A half century later, the whole world's been transformed—not just by the Pill but by the Cold War, the microchip, women's lib, and TV. My parents' lives have been reinvented as well, by two daughters and two dogs, Mom's college degree, the loss of three parents, and more. I haven't been privy to all of their years, but enough to know they've known their share of sorrow and grief, strife and struggle, of laughter and joy and reward. And while golden anniversaries are milestones, truly worthy of tributes and praise, theirs seems all the more so, given the fact that my mother was eighteen when she married my father, an "older man" of twenty-one.

My sister, my grandmother, and I have been planning a party to celebrate the occasion in style. Friends and family will gather together; there'll be champagne and memories and cake. We'll raise our glasses to the joy and good times my parents have known, to the fruits of their labor, their love. But I wonder how many of us will know in our hearts what the big day will feel like to them. How many of our marriages will endure as theirs has? How many of us can relate?

They were, of course, clueless about what it takes to hang in there through thick and thin. But they learned as they went, and they had enough glue to stick it out no matter what. They had the usual young married hassles: no money, two babies, one car. My father lived much of his life in that car, traveling throughout the Northeast. That he never much cared for his work didn't add to the harmony of his married life. Nor did his obsession with everything golf. Those years were no day at the beach.

But they helped pave the way for the life they have now, so in that sense, the years have been kind. Two grandchildren, early retirement, good health, and a place of their own in the sun. Their Florida home is a testament to the good life my parents now share, overlooking a golf course where my mother plays too, often putting my father to shame. None of us visit as much as we'd like, but we fly down whenever we can. And each time we do, we embark on a tour of their latest home furnishings.

The last time I went, they had bought a new print, a watercolor in muted pastels that depicted a couple out walking the beach, arm in arm, with their shoes in their hands. It reminded me of one of those soft-focus cards, with its idealized view of romance: a beautiful woman with long, flowing hair, and a broad-shouldered, wasp-waisted man. My mom said my father had chosen the print because "it reminds him of us." I looked at them standing there looking at me, then I looked at the painting again. To tell the truth, I couldn't see it at all. I mean, it was not even close. All manner of smart-ass remarks filled my head—the typical daughter's response—but in the end, I just nodded and kept my mouth shut. And looking back, I am glad that I did. Because it really doesn't matter whether I see the resemblance. What matters is that they both can. And that the image that sums up their marriage to them is that of a day at the beach.

Nancy Shulins

When neighbors of ours, Len and Carol, celebrated their fiftieth anniversary recently, I asked them the secret of their long, happy marriage. Given Carol's thoughtful expression and the time she took to consider the question, I was expecting the usual answer, about working together as a team, being willing to compromise, and treating each other with respect. Instead, I got this: "I keep a flyswatter on the dashboard of the car," Carol said, "and whenever Lenny does something I don't like, I whack him with it."

It's as good an answer as any, I suppose, because ultimately, who really knows? The love that holds people together for life is mysterious, elusive, and rare. Like snowflakes or humans, no two loves are alike; every couple must find their own way. It's that journey through life that we celebrate here, the one for which there is no map. The footprints we leave get erased by the tides, but the love we create never dies. As miraculous as the ocean, as mundane as a flyswatter, as singular as each one of us.

Multiply life by the power of two.

EMILY SALIERS

PERHAPS IT'S BECAUSE I never got to name babies, despite having their names all picked out. Or
maybe, since champagne's my beverage of choice, it's a
handy excuse to drink more. But whatever the reason, I
make a big deal of the process of choosing a name. I did
it again when my mate got his boat (which is formally
known as *Thin Ice*), dragging four friends, a cake, and
the ubiquitous drink on a voyage to christen the
"yacht."

Recently, having just about wrapped up this book,
my obsession kicked in yet again. My agent and editor
were both prodding me to come up with a suitable
name. The truth is, I'd tried for some months to think
up something witty, original, fun. So far, I'd failed mis-
erably, but then again, my attempts lacked the requisite
prop. This time would be different, I thought, as I
placed the fresh bottle to chill in the fridge. My hus-

band was still on *Thin Ice,* so to speak, so I had a bit of a wait. He returned rather late, looking sunburned and beat, and in desperate need of a bath.

Like a hyperactive border collie (redundant, I know), I herded him to the table instead and said, "It's time to come up with a name for my book, and nobody moves till we're done." He sighed and he shifted around in his chair, struggling valiantly to stay awake. A bevy of terrible names issued forth; I shall share a small sampling with you. "To Have and to Scold." "Doing Life." "Stuck With You." It was clear we were getting nowhere. "I Love You Like Crazy, but You're Making Me Nuts." (That was mine, and I liked it a lot.) By this time, of course, we were punchy as hell, and our efforts reflected our mood. "A Little Song, a Little Dance," I began, and my husband chimed right in on cue: "A Little Seltzer in Your Pants."

So we still had no name, but we were having fun, and as always, that counts for a lot. But sad to say, not quite enough in this case, since we hadn't managed to get the job done.

What's in a name, Shakespeare wanted to know. Everything, Will, in this case. It's the universe etched on the head of a pin stuck in something that can't be pinned down. Marriage, like life, is too fluid, too supple, too changeable to categorize. We can isolate moments to stick in a book, which is essentially what these essays are, but by the time the glue dries, we are already subtly somewhere—and somebody—else. The mere act of removing ourselves from the action to analyze what's going on will adversely affect the way our spouses act: the home version of the Butterfly Effect.

And yet, we who keep pinning our hopes on the hope that our love will forever endure cannot help but keep checking for signs of distress even when there are none to be found. Far be it for me, the Impending Doom Queen, to take issue with anyone else, but I do try to take frequent breaks from the task of overanalyzing my own married life in order to make an attempt to get on with the day-to-day living of it. And I hope you will, too, because that's where the magic of married life waits to be found—along with the romance, the laughter, the love, and the faith we all need when the magic seems lost. This book will help guide you, but ultimately you can't learn how to love from a book. And certainly not from the name of a book. Only loving someone teaches that.

I was starting to understand why I was having such an awful time naming my book. I turned to my husband to share this with him, this unparalleled enlightenment. My words seemed to come from a far deeper place than I'd ever tapped into before. I'd just reached the part about the Butterfly Effect when he did something that made me stop dead: he raised his left arm to his face in a gesture of boredom, dismissal, fatigue. That flick of the wrist deflated me like a hatpin deflates a balloon. I'd been having the greatest epiphany of my life—and he had been checking his watch! I turned on him then, and my voice reached new heights. I was practically screeching at him. To the point where it took half a minute or so for his rebuttal to finally get through.

It turned out I was wrong. He had not checked his watch. My white knight had been picking his nose. Which just meant that he hadn't stopped listening at all; he was still hanging in there with me.

There is no Hallmark card for a moment like this, no Shakespearean sonnet, no song. There is only the heart-swelling rush of pure love, and an insight that can't be denied: when you catch your mate picking his nose and rejoice, you've been married an awfully long time. And you'll probably stay married the rest of your life, which feels funny and great all at once.

Because loving one partner for life is what gives life its texture, its meaning, its joy. And while no one is ideal, there's a lot to be said for a someone who sometimes comes close. As I looked around the dining room then, all our things seemed to take on a life of their own. All the artifacts of our married life spoke to me of the moments and good times we've shared. His seabag on the floor, my saddle pad on the chair, our dog fast asleep at our feet. The stained glass we had searched for that hangs on the wall, the china displayed in the hutch. Even the most mundane, everyday things seemed invested with meaning somehow. The basket of laundry I had yet to fold overflowed with the clothes I've bought him. The boots he gave me for my birthday were still by the front door where I'd kicked them off. All this stuff that was his, mine, and ours added up to much more than the sum of their parts. As did we, as we struggled together to solve a dilemma that sharing had halved.

I've never been good at math, yet even I can't help but see what you get when you add it all up. You get life multiplied by the power of two, bound by laundry and love. Me and you.

The author wishes to acknowledge the following for their assistance in the writing of this book:

First and foremost, my heartfelt thanks to my wonderful agent, Joanna Pulcini at the Linda Chester Literary Agency, whose intelligence, enthusiasm, and vision have shaped this project from the start. Without her love, guidance, and support, I would never have written this book. I also wish to thank the agency staff, particularly Gary Jaffe and Kelly Smith, for efforts above and beyond the call of duty. And, of course, Linda herself, for believing in my talent and helping me plot a new course.

My gratitude to my delightful and talented editor, Diana Baroni at Warner Books, for her patience, dedication, and skill. I didn't know at the outset how lucky I was to have had my book land on this woman's desk. I do now. I also am greatly indebted to Publisher Jamie Raab for her enthusiasm and support, and to editorial assistant Molly Chehak; Chris Barba, director of sales and marketing; and Chris Dao in publicity.

My thanks to my parents and grandmother, whose long, happy marriages informed every page; to my sister, who brainstormed with me and contributed countless ideas; to my mother-in-law, Phyllis Curcio, and my sister-in-law, Claudia Berns, who read every word, more than once. And to my husband, who displayed so much grace and good humor at having his life become, literally, an open book.

My deepest appreciation to Claire, Celia, Amy, Alex, Janice, Sandy, Dolores, Arthur and Laura, John and Susan, John and Patti, Debbie and Barry, and Evan and Claudia, who gave me their input and entrusted me with their tales.

And finally, to the extraordinary women of Ladies' Night Out, who periodically dragged me away from these pages to tell the truth about husbands, and life.